Salmon Fishers of the Columbia

Salmon Fishers
of the
Columbia

Courtland L. Smith

OREGON STATE UNIVERSITY PRESS
CORVALLIS

Library of Congress Cataloging in Publication Data

Smith, Courtland L
    Salmon fishers of the Columbia.

    1. Pacific salmon fisheries—Columbia River—History. 2. Indians
of North America—Northwest, Pacific—Fishing—History.   3. Columbia River—IIistory.   I. Title.
SH348.S63   639′.27′55   79-10125
ISBN 0-87071-313-2

Contents

List of Figures

List of Tables

Acknowledgments

While investigating questions on limiting entry and fishermen's organizations for the Sea Grant Program, I discovered that problems discussed as needing solution in the 1970s were much like important problems in the salmon fishery of the 1880s. Thus, I collected historical information on salmon fishers, canners, fishery managers, and others associated with the canned salmon industry. While the industry changed dramatically in a century, the crucial resource management questions remained very much the same. I am most appreciative of the opportunity provided by the Sea Grant Program to pursue these historical questions emphasizing the recurrent nature of many public policy problems.

A postdoctoral fellowship at the Woods Hole Oceanographic Institution provided time to write this part of the Columbia River salmon story. I also benefited from the enthusiastic response of WHOI scientists and students to the segments of this story which I presented while there.

To assemble the historical summary, fishermen were interviewed. I relied more heavily, however, on archives preserved in many West Coast museums and libraries. Particularly helpful was Susan Suddeth of the Oregon Historical Society who introduced me to records on operations of the Columbia River Packers Association. These records covered CRPA's activities from the early 1900s to the 1920s. Bruce Bernie of the Astoria Public Library helped me to locate additional Columbia River Packers Association records stored there, as well as old issues of Astoria newspapers and other historic documents. Michael Naab at the Columbia River Maritime Museum, David Hall of the San Francisco Maritime Museum, George Abdill with the Douglas County Historical Museum, and Pat Brandt of the Oregon State Library all suggested relevant materials located in their collections. I also used collections located at the University of California Berkeley Bancroft Library, the University of Washington Library Special Collections, Seattle Museum of Science and Industry, Special Collections of the University of British Columbia, Special Collections at the University of Oregon, and the Oregon State Library.

All or portions of the manuscript have been read by several people. Each has made valuable comments and suggestions. Robert L. Hacker, author of a 1935 study on the Columbia River salmon fishery, read the entire manuscript and made detailed comments. Susan Peterson, anthropologist, and Fred Smith, economist, both made numerous useful suggestions. Shirley Hill, senior editor at the Oregon State University Press and member of an Oregon canning family, was particularly helpful in preparing the manuscript for publication. Kal Hatizkon, Angus McKay, Leah Smith, Linda Varsell Smith, Helen Varsell, and William Q. Wick each made suggestions which strengthened the manuscript.

I greatly appreciate responses of family, friends, and people to whom I told parts of this story. Their interest provided encouragement and made writing about the canned salmon industry a particularly enjoyable experience.

COURTLAND L. SMITH
Department of Anthropology
Oregon State University

Chapter 1/

Too Many Fishers

THIS IS A "fistory"—a history of a fishery. It focuses on growth and decline in the Columbia River canned salmon industry, which began in 1866. By the late 1880s, the Columbia River was the biggest salmon-producing area on the Pacific Coast. During the early 1900s, the salmon industry was Oregon's third largest, but by 1975 the amount of salmon canned dropped to a level less than the pack of 1867, the second year of the industry.

The story of the canned salmon industry, how it came about, grew, and then declined is told in the words of fishers, canners, merchants, consumers, and others associated with the fishery. Their remarks have been preserved in cannery records, letters, newspaper articles, and other publications.

Late in the eighteenth century Native Americans were the only fishers and fish processors. In the first part of the nineteenth century white explorers, traders, and settlers sought to profit from marketing Columbia River salmon to many parts of the world. Travelers' commentaries and records from this period indicate that these early efforts to market salmon were unsuccessful.

Then, in the 1860s, salmon canning was introduced on the Pacific Coast and a new industry was born. Government studies, cannery records, and accounts of the participants themselves are used to describe this early period. The new industry grew rapidly. Many became rich and reported on their success in canning salmon. But success proved to be the industry's worst enemy. Soon there were too many fishers, canners, and others seeking wealth and well-being from Columbia River salmon.

Competition for salmon predominated from the 1870s to the 1970s. Many groups looked to the salmon fishery to maintain or improve their well-being, and the resource could not meet all of their demands. The result was conflict—people fighting for a limited share of salmon. At times the conflicts erupted into physical violence, but usually the battle was more subtle. Economic conditions, innovations, regulations, ballot measures, and the courts were commonly the weapons for "fish fights."

❀   ❀   ❀   ❀

Columbia River salmon eggs hatch in streams, rivers, and, since 1877, in hatcheries. Juveniles migrate to the ocean and spend several years feeding there. Adult salmon return to their home streams and hatcheries to spawn. Throughout their lives' journey salmon are the prey of numerous creatures, not the least of whom are humans.

Humans are unique predators in a number of ways. They question the impacts they have on their prey. They support fishery managers who act as referees, trying to keep the various fishing groups from overexploiting the resource. Humans organize in groups to further their interests. These organizations are influential in determining the advantage of one group over another. A fishing organization may strongly support conservation measures. Its motivation, however, may be to exclude a competing group. Humans also develop the technology to increase salmon supplies by manipulating the life cycle of the fish.

Columbia River fishery management, as practiced through the first three-quarters of the twentieth century, dealt mainly with fishermen and fish. Yet a fishery is an industry composed of fishers, processors, merchants, and consumers. The actions and attitudes of all these people influence how a fishery operates and who will benefit from it. Further, a fishery is but one industry in a complex society. Agriculture, lumbering, electric power generation, manufacturing, city living, pollution abatement, and recreation all compete with fisheries for Columbia Basin waters and habitat.

Fishery management, then, is not solely concerned with fish. Its impacts are on people and the way they interact with one another. A fishery and fishery management activities are part of human communities. These communities are composed of many different people, each trying to attain a variety of benefits. The Columbia River salmon fishery is an example of the social, political, and economic processes that people used to gain these benefits.

A century of concern over who should be allowed to catch Columbia River salmon provides an illustration of competition for a scarce resource. From a historical perspective, this competition has been a persistent problem that seems to defy resolution. However, it also provides a perspective on the potentials for new methods of management.

❊   ❊   ❊   ❊

Limiting the number of fishermen so their harvest capacity would more closely match the quantity available was suggested as a solution to the demand for salmon in the 1970s. By 1975, Alaska, British Columbia, and Washington had programs to limit the number of salmon fishers. British Columbia's program was the oldest, implemented in 1968.

Many of the Oregon fishermen were skeptical about similar programs for their fishery, but they were also frustrated with the increasing restrictions on their fishing gear and time. Many wanted the number of fishers to be restricted by some program that would limit entry. Listening to them made it apparent that the critical problem was too many fishers and not enough fish. However, attempts to solve this problem have met with varying degrees of success. The reference "our fish" was a phrase common to all solutions suggested. Invariably, one group's solution involved limiting access of another group to the salmon resource. This was implied by, "They're taking our fish." "They" varied as one group after another attempted to make the salmon resource their own.

Salmon fishers of the early 1970s can be divided into three general categories—professional, part-timers, and sport-commercial. *Professional* fishermen depended on fishing for most of their income and fished full time within the limits of management regulations and weather conditions. *Part-timers* were fishers seriously interested in fishing, but only as a part-time activity. Usually they mixed fishing with other occupations. Management regulations restricted many of them to only part-time fishing. For those in other occupations, who could get time off from their jobs, the management regulations created new opportunities to supplement income. The third class, *sport-commercial*, included fishers who typically fished only on weekends and during vacations. Most of them had previously fished for recreation but depended on other occupations for their livelihood. In the early 1970s about 10 percent of the salmon fishers were professional, 30 to 40 percent part-timers, and 50 to 60 percent sport-commercial.

Commercial fishers were not the only ones seeking salmon. Thousands of recreation anglers purchased trips on charter boats or used their own boats to fish at sea, in estuaries, and on rivers. Others fished for salmon from jetties, docks, and riverbanks. The expenditures of the recreation angler contributed to the recreational industry and to the receipts of local tackle shops, marinas, restaurants, and motels. Fishery managers cut recreation seasons and reduced bag limits when fish runs were inadequate. Here, too, people worried about the problem of too many fishers.

All fishers expressed concern with problems facing the salmon fishery. They desired more action on problems such as resource depletion caused by pollution, dams, and overfishing. They wanted lawmakers to more carefully consider the impacts of newly imposed governmental regulations. Some wanted more research on harvest technologies, others on hatchery development.

Opinions of commercial fishers on limiting entry reflected their success, expectations, perceived adequacy of the fish resource, and definition of a good society. About 40 percent expressed opposition to limiting who could fish. They felt that in a free enterprise system each person deserved the opportunity to make a living. Some also were worried about opportunities for their children. Others were concerned about losing the flexibility to move from place to place and fishery to fishery.

Those who wanted to limit the number of fishers were most concerned about limiting the effectiveness of their competitors. Several said, "Why regulate us when the Soviets are free to fish?" Fishermen with larger boats favored limitations to exclude small boats, and those with small boats opposed any limitation on vessel size. Some fishermen wanted to keep large out-of-state boats off their homegrounds.

A program that required earning a certain percent of income from fishing to get a license was mentioned most by fishers who favored limiting entry. This would separate fishermen dependent upon fishing as an occupation from those who fished to supplement other incomes. The recommended percent of income varied, but it always exceeded 50 percent. Those fishing full time attempted to eliminate part-time and sport-commercial fishers. Those in the latter two categories responded by saying, "America was built on free enterprise." Others said, "I don't catch enough fish to matter. Those who have made it always want to regulate out the others." Several noted, "It's a big ocean. With the existing technology for harvesting fish, all fishermen are needed to achieve an adequate harvest."

Professional fishers were concerned about the effect the nonprofessionals would have on fish prices and by their lack of support of fishermen's organizations. Professional fishermen argued that even when the nonprofessionals supported the professionals on price, the fact that the fish processors knew nonprofessionals were competing for the resource adversely affected prices received and negotiations to obtain a "fair" price. Further, the professional fishers criticized the nonprofessional fishers for getting in the way, having a low investment in their equipment, and not being concerned with the fishing industry.

A few fishermen reduced the issue of limiting entry to a simple equation: "If you have a big boat, you favor it. If you have a small boat, you're against it." Others were penetratingly perceptive about the diverse impacts of university research programs. Commenting on the relationship between programs to stimulate gear development and studies on limiting entry, one fisherman said, "You university guys are working against yourselves, aren't you? One guy is stimulating people to go fishing, and you are trying to find out how to stop them."

One day an old Columbia River gillnetter responded to the question, "What should be done about the problem of too many fishermen and too few fish?" Continuing to prepare his net, he remarked sorrowfully, "It's too late." He described the fishery in 1917 when he had entered as a part-timer. For the first 10 years he was a logger as well as a fisherman. He quit logging in 1927 to take up fishing as a full-time occupation.

If it is too late, as the gillnetter said, can there ever be a solution to the problem of too many fishers? What stimulated more people to fish? The gillnetter's remark implied that once there was a time when the problem could have been solved. When was that time?

◦   ◦   ◦   ◦

Accounts of the Columbia River salmon fishery show that the need for limiting the number of fishermen was recognized in the 1880s. In 1884, meetings were held among canners to curtail the fishery. The *Oregonian* reported that "few could be found willing to adopt the proposed means—that of reducing the number of boats employed, averaging them with the capacity of the canneries."[1] For the 1885 season the *Oregonian* reported, "As in the preceding years the last was no exception, and there was the usual talk of limiting the pack to a quantity below that of 1884."[2] The editor of the *Weekly Astorian* wrote on August 20, 1887, that "to cut down the number of boats in the river at least one-half, just as many salmon would be caught as under the present ruinous way of carrying on business." In 1896, Astoria gillnetters tried limiting their numbers as part of the strike settlement. They wanted canners to take the twine for knitting nets away from the "floating element of the craft, who have no home ties in the city, and who only come during the season to work."[3]

Many times since the 1880s, groups of Columbia River salmon fishermen have used force against one another. At other times, these fish fights were arbitrated by citizens at the ballot box. Fishery managers regulated the gear used and the times fished. Fishermen, however, reached out into the ocean beyond the manager's scope of authority. Economic conditions, too, influenced who fished. No matter what the circumstance—fish fights, ballot measures, regulation, or economic conditions—the problem of too many fishers persisted.

Since the mid-1930s, problems with Columbia River salmon runs also have been attributed to "the dams." Dams are good scapegoats. These concrete monoliths serve as tributes to a technocratic age. They cannot talk, and they weather the abuse heaped on them while continuing to slave for those of us who benefit from their power.

To blame "the dams," however, is to miss the point. The dams are merely instruments of a technocratic society. Many benefit from their presence. Others bear the costs brought on by the ecological changes caused by damming a river. Electricity, water storage, and flood control measures benefit vast numbers of citizens. One of the costs of these benefits is modification of a free-flowing river into a series of slack water pools. This habitat is not preferred by salmon, so why should it be preferred by those who depend on salmon for their livelihood?

A dam is not a problem because it is a dam. A dam is a problem because it creates benefits for some and hardships for others. The dams are not "the problem." They are merely symptomatic of a problem with interactions among people. Nor is this a new problem. For more than one hundred years, access to Columbia River salmon has involved conflict among various groups who wanted to increase their own benefits. Dams, fish fights, regulations, economic conditions, and many other factors have helped some groups and hurt others. Once there are more fishers than fish, people use a variety of means to increase their advantage over others.

[1] *Oregonian,* January 1, 1885.
[2] *Oregonian,* January 1, 1886.
[3] *Daily Astorian,* May 8, 1896.

Chapter 2/

First Fishers

WHEN WHITE SETTLERS arrived in the Columbia River basin at the beginning of the nineteenth century, the Indians already relied heavily on the river's salmon runs. A Native American population of 50,000 caught an estimated 18 million pounds of Columbia River salmon each year. This figure is based on an average daily consumption of one pound of salmon per person.[1]

With the influx of settlers, the Native American population declined, principally due to settler-introduced diseases. The 1851 *Annual Report of the Commissioner of Indian Affairs* estimated 8,280 Columbia River Indians, one-sixth of the precontact population.[2] Sometime during the 1840s the settler and Native American populations were equal in size, about 10,000 each. In terms of dynamics, however, the settlers were rapidly increasing while the reverse was true of Native Americans.

Early explorers noted Native American fisheries all along the Columbia and its tributaries.

Nearly half the Native American population were Chinook peoples living along and adjacent to the lower Columbia River. The next largest groups were the Klikitat, Yakima, Wanapum, and Palus, living along the mid-Columbia in the vicinity of Celilo Falls. Together, these peoples comprised more than half of the basin's 50,000 inhabitants.[3] Other groups were spread throughout the basin. Many, such as the Nez Perce, migrated widely. When hunting was poor they would come west to Willamette Falls to catch salmon in the early runs. The Great Basin peoples, residing east of the Cascade Mountains, lived on a three-part economy—salmon, digging for roots, and hunting. These Indians shifted between subsistence activities, depending on the season of the year and the availability of fish, roots, and game.[4]

In addition to exploiting the local subsistence base, Native Americans of the Columbia traded for a variety of goods. The mouth of the river was the center of three trade routes: one was coastwise, one came from central Washington through the Cascades, and the most important went east along the Columbia River and extended out onto the Great Plains. A north-south route extended from Kettle Falls, near the Canadian border, into southern Oregon and passed through Celilo Falls.

[1] Gordon W. Hewes, "Aboriginal Use of Fishery Resources in Northwestern North America," Ph.D. dissertation, Department of Anthropology, University of California, Berkeley, 1947, pp. 214-228; and Deward E. Walker, Jr., *Mutual Cross-Utilization of Economic Resources in the Plateau: An Example from Aboriginal Nez Perce Fishing Practices,* Washington State University, Laboratory of Anthropology Report of Investigations No. 41 (1967), p. 23.

[2] Anson Dart, "Report No. 68," *Report of the Commissioner of Indian Affairs, Department of the Interior* (Washington, D.C., 1851), First Session, Thirty-second Congress, Serial Set No. 613, pp. 477-478.

[3] Hewes, 1947, pp. 227-228 (see note 1).
[4] Walker, 1967, pp. 9, 14 (see note 1).

The lower Columbia Chinook were central to many trade transactions. Chinook Jargon was a trade language for 100 different Pacific Northwest groups. The dentalium shell, *Dentalium preiosum,* from the Straits of Juan de Fuca, was the medium of exchange.[5] Dried salmon, pulverized salmon, smelt, seal, blubber, and fish products flowed east along the Columbia. Wood products were also traded east. From the Great Basin and as far as the Great Plains came roots, dried meat, bone, horses, and skins of deer, elk, and buffalo.

*   *   *   *

Knowledge of the Native American cultures comes from accounts of travelers and anthropologists. The accounts are fragmentary because large numbers of Indians had died before any attempt was made to learn the nature of their cultures. Available data show that salmon were an important part of these cultures. The Indians' oral literature suggests that they believed in a time when "animals walked about as men, though having approximately the same mental and, to a large extent, physical characteristics as now." But things were not as they should be and "it was necessary for a culture-hero or transformer to rectify the weak points in creation."[6] Coyote was the miracle transformer, but according to anthropologist Edward Sapir, Coyote was not a chief or hero—that special position was reserved for Eagle and Salmon.

Sapir collected Wishram texts on the Yakima Reservation during the summer of 1905. The Wishram were a Chinook group living in the vicinity of the Cascades of the Columbia River. Sapir's informant, Louis Simpson, after three-quarters of a century's experience in two cultures, believed in the "truth of all the myths he narrated." Simpson felt that Coyote was equivalent to Christ, since both had "appeared in this world in order to better the lot of mankind."[7]

Coyote did much to improve conditions for the people in the Columbia Basin. He created the Columbia River and the fish in it by making an outlet to a pond where two women kept fish. Coyote said to the women, "Now by what right, perchance, would you two keep the fish to yourselves?" Coyote told of the coming of people to the region, and he said of the salmon, "those fish will be the people's food."[8] He provided the people with mouths and then taught them how to catch and cook salmon.

Oral literature recorded by anthropologists indicates the importance of salmon throughout the culture of Columbia River peoples. Most texts include a salmon story. The salmon story centers around the activities of Salmon in avenging the death of his father, a death attributed to the mischief of Coyote, Skunk (sometimes referred to as Badger), and five Wolves. In the story, Salmon meets and travels with his father's wife, whom he punishes for disgracing his father. Later he restores her as Dove. Salmon has the power to change his form, perform feats of strength, and transform physical phenomena.[9]

As a hero, Salmon was capable of superhuman performances. For example, Salmon created Dove by pouring oil over her five times. "She had no hair at all and they brought her home lean." After Salmon's treatment, "Her body was beautiful in every way."[10] Another time, in competing to break a pair of antlers in order to marry the chief's daughter, all the animals tried and failed. "Now there was one person in the house whose body was full of sores and boils." Blue-Jay said, "Let him try what he can do, the one whose body is sore all over." When all the animals had tried and failed, the one with sores rose and shook his body, his blanket, and his hair. He became very beautiful, and the people saw that he was Salmon. Salmon went to the mid-

---

[5] Verne F. Ray, "Lower Chinook Ethnographic Notes," *University of Washington Publications in Anthropology* 7 (1938), p. 100.

[6] Edward Sapir, "Preliminary Report on the Language and Mythology of the Upper Chinook," *American Anthropologist* 9 (1907), pp. 533-544.

[7] Edward Sapir, *Wishram Texts,* (Washington: American Ethnological Society, 1909), Vol. 2, p. xi.

[8] Sapir, 1909, p. 7 (see note 7).

[9] Franz Boas, *Chinook Texts,* Bureau of American Ethnology Bulletin No. 20 (1894), pp. 77-87; Sapir, 1909, pp. 49-65 (see note 7) and Leslie Spier and Edward Sapir, "Wishram Ethnography," *University of Washington Publications in Anthropology* 3 (1930), p. 273.

[10] Sapir, 1909, p. 65 (see note 7).

dle of the house, "took up the antlers and broke them . . . into five pieces and threw them down."[11]

＊　＊　＊　＊

Native American fishermen saw Salmon as being immortal. Because of this, they believed that salmon consciously allowed themselves to be caught. Many forms of gear were used to catch salmon. These included traps, seines, weirs, baskets, spears, and hook and line.[12] Coyote was the principal teacher in gear construction and use.

The method which attracted the most attention among non-Indians was the dipnet, a device that was fished in fast water. The net was hung on a 4-foot-diameter hoop attached to a 30-foot pole.[13] The net was made to slide on the hoop so as to close into a bag with the weight of a salmon. It was usually fished blind, which means the fisherman could not see the fish. Dipping platforms were built over eddies. The swirling water caused the bag of net to flare. When the fisherman felt something strike his net, he rapidly pulled the net straight up out of the water.

Dipnetting was observed by early explorers at Willamette Falls, Spokane Falls, Kettle Falls on the Columbia near the Canadian border, and Salmon Falls on the Snake River. The most important fishing sites were the Cascades of the Columbia, 150 miles upriver, and Celilo Falls, 200 miles from the mouth. These fishing grounds attracted many tribes. The rapids of the river concentrated the salmon and also concentrated the fishers. Sometimes as many as 3,000 men, women, and children gathered at the height of a run.[14] Not all the activity was fishing. Alexander Ross, traveling through the Cascades of the Columbia in August 1811, complained of the difficulty his party had in obtaining salmon when trading with the Indians. "For every fisherman there are fifty idlers, and all fish caught were generally devoured

[11] Boas, 1894, p. 78 (see note 9).
[12] Hewes, 1947, Figures 1-169 (see note 1).
[13] Captain Charles Wilkes, *Narrative of the United States Exploring Expedition During the Years 1838, 1839, 1840, 1841 and 1842* (Philadelphia: Lea & Blanchard, 1845), Vol. 4, p. 345.
[14] Alexander Ross, *Adventures of the First Settlers on the Oregon or Columbia River* (London: Smith, Elder and Co., 1849), p. 117.

Wishram dipnetter, 1909 (Edward S. Curtis photo, Tozzer Library, Harvard University).

on the spot; so that the natives of the place seldom lay up their winter stock until the gambling season is over, and their troublesome visitors are gone."[15]

Captain Charles Wilkes visited Willamette Falls in 1841 at the height of the dipnetting. Fishing patterns there were the same as at Celilo, Spo-

[15] Ross, 1849, Vol. 4, p. 118 (see note 14).

Dipnetting at the narrows of the Columbia River, 1880s (Henry Wood Elliott drawing, courtesy of Robert L. Hacker).

kane, Salmon, and other falls and fast waters along the Columbia River and its tributaries. The Indians fishing there first "rig out two stout poles, long enough to project over the foaming cauldron, and secure their larger ends to the rocks. On the outer end they make a platform for the fisherman to stand on." Wilkes observed of the dipnetting, "They throw it into the foam as far up the stream as they can reach, and it being then quickly carried down, the fish who are running up in a contrary direction are caught. Sometimes twenty large fish are taken by a single person in an hour."[16]

[16] Wilkes, 1845, Vol. 4, p. 345 (see note 13).

On the Columbia the platforms for dipnetting were prepared in the summer, when the river's freshet was over. Louis Simpson told Sapir that a "workingman," someone who is very strong, set the poles for the platform. To protect against drowning, "the man is tied with a rope about his belly."[17] The end of the rope was tied to the shore. Several men owned these fishing sites in common, and their families fished there year after year. Each site had an overseer who was usually a chief or headman.[18] Other dipnetters could fish from a platform with permission from its overseer.

When a fish was caught, it belonged to the man fishing from the platform at that time. If the dipnetter let a salmon lie, one of the old men watching the fishing "kills them, and obtains them for himself," said Simpson. If the dipnetter "slaps himself on his buttocks" as he catches the salmon, said Simpson, "those fish belong to himself."[19]

At Kettle Falls, near the Canadian border, a large basket was used to catch the salmon. The basket was supported by two long poles and fixed in the rocks. According to Wilkes, "This basket, during the fishing season, is raised three times a day, and at each haul, not infrequently contains three hundred fine fish."[20] At Salmon Falls on the Snake River, Robert Stuart came upon "about one hundred lodges of Shoshones busily engaging in killing and drying fish . . . the Indians swim to the center of the falls, where some station themselves on rocks, and others stand to their waists in the water, all armed with spears, with which they assail the salmon as they leap, or fall back exhausted." The catch was referred to as "an incessant slaughter."[21] The spearing of salmon was usually restricted to the autumn of the year. Spears were two pronged.

Wherever there were sandy shoals, the seine was a common form of gear used. In June 1853 Swan observed the Chinooks near the mouth of the

[17] Sapir, 1909, p. 107 (see note 7).
[18] Walker, 1967, pp. 8, 14-15 (see note 1).
[19] Sapir, 1909, p. 187 (see note 7).
[20] Wilkes, 1845, Vol. 4, p. 444 (see note 13).
[21] Washington Irving, *Astoria or Anecdotes of an Enterprise Beyond the Rocky Mountains,* ed. Edgeley W. Todd (Norman: University of Oklahoma Press, 1964), p. 373.

Wishram spearing salmon, 1909 (Edward S. Curtis photo, Tozzer Library, Harvard University).

river using seines constructed of a "twine spun from the fibres of spruce roots . . . sticks of dry cedar are used for floats, and the weights at the bottom are round beach pebbles, about a pound each notched to keep them from slipping from their fastenings, and securely held with withes of cedar firmly twisted and woven into the foot-rope of the net." The net was controlled by three men, and fishing started "at the top of high-water, just as the tide begins to ebb . . . Two persons get into the canoe, on the stern of which is coiled the net on a frame made for the purpose, resting on the canoe's gunwale." The canoe was paddled upstream, close to the beach, where the current was not strong. "The net is carried down the stream," observed Swan, "by the force of the ebb, about the eighth of a mile, the man on shore walking along slowly, holding on to the line till the others are ready, when all haul in together." Sometimes several hauls were made without success, but "in

Salmon seining at **Chinook Beach** (James G. Swan drawing, *The Northwest Coast; or, Three Years' Residence in Washington Territory*, 1857, p. 106).

seasons of plenty, great hauls are often made, and frequently a hundred fine fish of various sizes are taken at one cast of the seine."[22]

Upstream, the Wishram used seines 100 feet long and 12 feet deep, tied from a "selected flax fiber." The mesh of the net was 3 to 4 inches wide. The floats were wooden and the stone sinkers weighed 3 pounds.[23]

Coyote, the miracle performer, taught the Wishram how to make the salmon trap. "He began to twine cords of hazel-brush," said Louis Simpson, "and when the trap was finished he hung it over the riffle." Coyote instructed the trap to call him when it was filled with salmon. Soon he heard a call, "I am now filled! I am now filled!" Coyote went to the trap and found that it was full. He called the people from the village and distributed two salmon to each. "But there were not enough, and he set the trap again and again, five times in all, and by that time the people had learned how to use it, and how to make one."[24]

One of the most common types of gear, especially on smaller tributaries of the Columbia, was the weir. Issac Stevens, who negotiated the treaties between the United States and the Indian nations, observed in 1854 a Pend d'Oreille weir on Clark's River near the place where it divides into sections separating three large islands. "One of these streams is wide, shallow, and swift; here the Indians annually construct a fence which reaches across the stream and guides the fish into a weir or rack, where they are caught in great numbers."[25]

[22] James G. Swan, *The Northwest Coast; or, Three Years' Residence in Washington Territory* (New York: Harper & Brothers, 1857), pp. 103-107.

[23] Spier and Sapir, 1930, p. 116 (see note 9).

[24] Sapir, 1909, p. 27 (see note 7).

[25] Issac I. Stevens, "Report No. 86," in *Report of the Commissioner of Indian Affairs, Department of the Interior* (Washington, D.C., 1854), Second Session, Thirty-third Congress, Serial Set No. 777, p. 422.

Nez Perce weir (drawing from Deward E. Walker, Jr., *Mutual Cross-Utilization of Economic Resources in the Plateau,* 1967, p. 27).

Having this assortment of gear, Native American fishers were well equipped to catch salmon in the various conditions of the river. In fact, their gear encompassed a range of variability comparable to that of the white fishers who exploited the salmon resources as a commercial enterprise.

✿   ✿   ✿   ✿

Indian fishers felt a oneness with the salmon, and this oneness is reflected in the procedure for getting runs of salmon. Franz Boas' informant, Charles Cultee, told of a time when the Chinook people were starving. "They tried to catch salmon in the dipnet, but they did not kill anything." They went upstream to the Clatsop and exchanged fern and rush roots for a little dry salmon and salmon skins. The Clatsop, however, humiliated the people by telling them if they came again to exchange, "we will cohabit with your women." Humiliated, the people's leader did not eat for days. His younger

brother, with the help of Iqamiā'tix, the fishermen's guardian spirit, was able to kill a salmon. The people decided to eat the salmon, and the young man who had been guided by Iqamiā'tix ordered the heating of stones. The hot stones were put in a kettle, and then the salmon, whole and uncut, was added. One old man nudged another and said, "Why do they treat the salmon in that way?" The other said, "Be quiet, do not disturb our young men. You will learn in due time what they are going to do with this salmon." Instead of eating the salmon, which had cooked for a long time in the kettle, the Indians placed the kettle in a fishing canoe. "Five men were in the canoe—four youths and the one whose guardian spirit helped him to obtain salmon." They paddled to the center of the river. "Then they took the kettle and poured the salmon and the stones into the water." As darkness approached, the young man instructed the people to set their nets. "When it grew day their canoes

The 1855 treaty provided for fishing in the "usual and accustomed places" (Oregon Department of Transportation).

were full of salmon ... Thus, the man who had Iqamiā'tix for his guardian spirit obtained salmon."[26]

There were also appropriate procedures for treating the first salmon caught so as to preserve the run. Coyote was the one who learned these traditions and then taught them to the people. Coyote was a trickster who gave the impression of impatience. He could learn the traditions only bit by bit because each time he heard some of the

tradition he cut off the instruction. When Coyote applied what he was taught, he found that he was only partially successful. Irritated by his lack of success, he would defecate and say to his excrements, "Why have the salmon disappeared?" To which his excrements would invariably reply, "Oh, you with bandy legs, you have no sense."[27]

Coyote went to fish for silverside salmon, but was not successful. On accosting his excrement, he was instructed, "When the first silver-side salmon

[26] Boas, 1894, pp. 232-233 (see note 9).

[27] Boas, 1894, p. 101 (see note 9).

is killed it must not be cut. It must be split along its back and roasted. It must not be steamed. Only when they go up river then they may be steamed." Coyote then caught three silversides and prepared them as he was instructed. The next day, however, he got no silversides. His excrement informed him, "When the first silver-side salmon are killed, spits must be made, one for the head, one for the back, one for the roe, one for the body. The gills must be burnt." The next day he killed three salmon and prepared them as instructed. The following day he caught 10, but the next morning he caught none. Confronting his excrement, he was instructed, "When the first silver-side salmon are killed, they are not left raw. All must be roasted. When many are caught, they must all be roasted before you go to sleep." Coyote fished successfully. He taught the people how to catch and prepare salmon. He told of taboos on who could eat salmon. "If a man who prepares corpses eats a silver-side salmon, they shall disappear at once." The salmon also would disappear if eaten by a murderer, menstruating woman, or a girl who had just reached maturity.[28]

Then Coyote went to catch chinook salmon with a net he had constructed. He was unsuccessful, and he defecated and spoke to his excrements. They scolded him, "Do you think their taboo is the same as that of the silver-side salmon?" Thus, Coyote learned a new set of taboos for catching salmon. First he was told, "You must not step over your net. When the first salmon are killed, they are not cut until the afternoon." Next he was scolded, "Never bail out your canoe. When you come home and cut the salmon, you must split it at the sides and roast the belly and back on separate double spits." Third, "When you kill a salmon you must never strike it with a stick. When they may be boiled, then you may strike it with a stick." Fourth, "When you have killed many salmon, you must never carry them outside the house. You must roast and eat them at the same place. When part is left you must stay at the same place." Fifth, "When you go fishing and it is ebb-tide early in the morning, you must lay your net before sunrise." These and many other instructions were given to Coyote,

and he showed the people so they "shall always do in the same manner."[29]

＊　　＊　　＊　　＊

The Native Americans had an effective way of storing salmon. They dried the salmon and then pounded them into a fine powder between two stones. Northwestern explorers Lewis and Clark observed this process and noted in their journal for October 22, 1805, that the powder was "put into a species of basket neatly made of grass and rushes better than two feet long and one foot diameter, which basket is lined with the skin of salmon stretched and dried for the purpose." The pemmican preserved in this way was very sweet tasting and "thus preserved those fish may be kept sound and sweet several years."[30] The pemmican, Lewis and Clark noted, was traded with Chinook peoples who lived near the mouth of the Columbia and were "excessively fond of the pounded fish having frequently asked us for some of it."[31]

Eastern U.S. and European markets had not had the experience of tasting pemmican. Early white traders on the Columbia tried to market salmon in a form that would be palatable to those of Euro-American backgrounds. This was unsuccessful, as reflected in a *San Francisco Bulletin* article of the 1850s. "The efforts to export salmon in barrels have not, so far as we can learn, been very successful." The article continued, "They, being very fat, do not keep well, and when the packages after the long voyage around the Horn are opened, they are not in good merchantable order."[32] Canning was the process that made the salmon resource marketable.

Louis Simpson told about a phophecy of whites coming to the Columbia. An old man, who learned of their coming in a dream one night, said, "Soon all sorts of strange things will come." He said, "They will bring to us something which you just have to point at anything moving way yonder, and

[28] Boas, 1894, pp. 101-102 (see note 9).
[29] Boas, 1894, pp. 103-105 (see note 9).
[30] Reuben Gold Thwaites, *Original Journals of the Lewis and Clark Expedition, 1804-1806* (New York: Dodd, Mead & Company, 1905), Vol. 3, p. 148.
[31] Thwaites, 1905, Vol. 3, p. 344 (see note 30).
[32] *San Francisco Bulletin*, n.d., located in Bancroft Scraps (Berkeley, Bancroft Library, University of California), Vol. 33, p. 4.

it will fall right down and die." This, it turned out, was the gun. He prophesied buckets for cooking, pieces of wood which make fire, and different animals.[33] The whites also brought diseases that killed many of the people. They brought new ways of using the salmon for trade, increasing demands on the salmon resource, and new attitudes about how natural resources should be sold to others for a profit. The whites brought a whole new culture to the Columbia, a culture based on different premises and different ways of doing things.

One of the most important cultural differences introduced by the whites was in attitudes toward ownership of land and resources. The Native Americans had territories to which various tribes claimed priority rights. They did not, however, have the concept of private ownership of land and resources. As Coyote said, these "fish will be the people's food."

As the number of white settlers grew, they demanded title to the tribal lands. In 1855, Washington Territory's Governor, Isaac Stevens, made treaties with many tribes in the Northwest. The procedure and treaty were very nearly the same in each case. From May 28 to June 11, 1855, Stevens met at Walla Walla with the tribes of the mid-Columbia. Lack of a common language caused a problem at these meetings, and Stevens appeared to be talking down to the tribal chiefs, referring to them over and over as "my children."[34]

Stevens proposed to provide the Indians with two reservations. In describing these reservations Stevens said, "We think they are large enough to furnish each man and each family with a farm, and grazing for all your animals. There is plenty of salmon on these Reservations."[35] Also promised were schools, mills, roads, supplies, and $500 a year for 20 years to each tribe's head chief. "You will be allowed to go to the usual fishing places," said Stevens, "and fish in common with the Whites."[36]

Many chiefs spoke out against the proposal. Stachas asked, "If your mothers were here in this country who gave you birth, and suckled you and while you were sucking some person came and took away your mother and left you alone and sold your mother, how would you feel then?" He answered his question, "This is our mother country as if we drew our lives from her."[37] Owhi questioned, "Shall I steal this land and sell it? . . . Shall I give the lands that are part of my body and leave myself poor and destitute?"[38]

The proposed reservations were too small, and the chiefs convinced Stevens to designate a third one. On June 9, a reservation was added for the Umatillas, Cayuse, and Walla Wallas. This, together with a reservation for the Yakimas and tribes to join them and one for the Nez Perce and tribes to join them, gave the Native Americans 13 percent of the 60,000 square miles they once roamed. The chiefs were promised by General Palmer, "You will not be required to go onto this reservation till our chief, the President, and his council sees this piece of paper and says it is good; and we build the houses, the mills and the blacksmith shop." In exchange for these promises Palmer told the chiefs, "We want you to allow the white people to come and settle in the country anywhere outside the reservation."[39]

Many chiefs were not satisfied, saying that the reservations were too small. Despite dissatisfaction, most of the chiefs signed "because they were told that their lands would be overrun by white settlers if they refused the treaty proposals."[40] From past experience the chiefs knew this threat to be a very real possibility.

---

[33] Sapir, 1909, pp. 220, 231 (see note 7).

[34] From a true copy of the official proceedings on file at the Nez Perce tribal headquarters and reprinted in Allen P. Slickpoo, Sr., and Deward E. Walker, Jr., *Noon Nee-Me-Poo, Culture and History of The Nez Perces* (Nez Perce Tribe of Idaho, 1973), pp. 83-142.

[35] Slickpoo and Walker, 1973, p. 110 (see note 34).

[36] Slickpoo and Walker, 1973, p. 112 (see note 34).
[37] Slickpoo and Walker, 1973, p. 116 (see note 34).
[38] Slickpoo and Walker, 1973, p. 120 (see note 34).
[39] Slickpoo and Walker, 1973, p. 127 (see note 34).
[40] Slickpoo and Walker, 1973, p. 142 (see note 34).

Chapter 3/

The Innovators

TREATIES ALLOWED Indians and white settlers to fish in common for salmon. In the 1860s, Columbia River salmon resources were adequate to serve the needs of both. Many settlers had more than their fill of salmon, which, along with potatoes, were staples of their wintertime diet.[1] The salmon resource was perceived as inexhaustible.

Some settlers saw more than subsistence in the salmon. They envisioned riches that could be gained from trade and commerce. Several tried to market salmon, but means of preservation were inadequate.

The first attempt to market salmon—shipment of barrels of salted salmon to Hawaii, the Atlantic Coast, and Europe—was not particularly successful. An article in the *San Francisco Bulletin* explained that salmon, "being very fat, do not keep well." The *Bulletin* went on to suggest drying or smoking, but "very little encouragement has been extended to this way of preparing salmon for market."[2]

Canning salmon was the process that enabled transportation over long distances, storage for long periods without spoiling, and palatability to consumers. Hapgood, Hume and Company introduced salmon canning on the Pacific Coast in 1864. The company first canned salmon from the Sacramento River, but moved to the Columbia River in 1866 because of overfishing, hydraulic mining, and stream obstructions in the Sacramento River area.

The new industry on the Columbia River created several problems that surfaced in the 1880s. Salmon trade and commerce greatly increased the number of people who depended on salmon for their subsistence. Initially, the quantity of salmon was adequate to meet the consumers' demand, and several early canners became wealthy. Success, however, does not go unrecognized, and many more canners came to share in the profits. The canners competed for fishermen to provide fish, and fish prices increased. They also competed for consumers, resulting in a decline in price of their product. In this squeeze between increased costs for fish and lower prices for canned salmon, only the canners who could find new markets, new processing techniques, and new harvest methods survived.

❖   ❖   ❖   ❖

Canning was nurtured in the French Revolution when Napoleon offered a prize of 12,000 francs to the person who could devise a way to store food for his sailors at sea. The prize was claimed by Nicholas Appert in 1809. Appert had begun his experiments to preserve food in 1806. His method of preservation was to cook and seal

[1] "Mr. Smith's Address, He Tells of Early Times in Oregon," *Morning Oregonian*, December 18, 1899.
[2] Located in Bancroft Scraps, n.d. (Berkeley, Bancroft Library, University of California), Vol. 33, p. 4.

foods in glass jars. He published the results of his work in 1810 in a book entitled, *Book for All Households on the Art of Preserving Animal and Vegetable Substances*. In 1819 Thomas Kensett introduced canning in the United States, and tin cans were substituted for glass in 1839.[3] That same year, Delaware oysters were preserved in cans. Andrew S. Hapgood, the canning specialist for Hapgood, Hume and Company, obtained his canning expertise when canning spread from New Brunswick into his native state of Maine.

In its first year of operation, Hapgood, Hume and Company was located on the Sacramento River and canned 2,000 cases of salmon.[4] Hydraulic mining, overfishing, and destruction of spawning habitats made the Sacramento unsuitable for continuing business. Furthermore, Columbia River salmon were reported to be larger and better. The company moved to the unspoiled and relatively uninhabited lower Columbia River in 1866. Here the annual salmon runs were described as "abundant," "limitless," and "undiminishing."

The exact date of arrival is not known, but Hapgood and the Hume brothers—George, William, and R. D.—came to the Columbia in late 1865. R. D. Hume, in his reflections of the Columbia during that first winter, wrote: "It rained forty days and forty nights without interruption." The winter was spent mending nets and making cans, which at that time were all cut and soldered by hand. Hume said that it was a "very lonely place there, the nearest neighbor being three miles off."[5]

Several salt salmon fisheries are mentioned in R. D. Hume's writings. The salt salmon trade had begun in the 1820s. Records show that in 1829 Captain Dominis purchased salmon from the Indians at three tobacco leaves per fish and packed the salmon in rum barrels.[6]

Others also tried to make packing salted salmon in barrels a commercial enterprise. They included the Hudson's Bay Company, Andrew Wyeth, John H. Couch, Kenneth McKay, Philip Foster, and captains Chapman and Lament.[7] By 1835, three to four thousand barrels were shipped annually to the Hawaiian Islands. The Hudson's Bay Company was the biggest shipper.[8]

However, the salt salmon fishery met with only limited success. Often the salmon arrived at their destination in unmarketable condition. In 1844 Oregon City merchant Philip Foster, who shipped shingles and salmon to Hawaii from 1843 to 1848, received a report from his broker, J. N. Colcord, noting that most of the barrels in a recent shipment "were rusty and not full." Barrels that arrived in good condition commanded a price of $8 to $10. Shipping costs were $2 a barrel. Foster's trade with Colcord ended unsuccessfully in 1848, with Foster in debt $435.29.[9]

Competition between trading companies was another reason for lack of success in the salt salmon trade. At Sauvie Island, Andrew Wyeth's Columbia River Fishing and Trading Company faced competition from John McLoughlin at the Hudson's Bay Company. According to historian Hubert Bancroft, "McLoughlin was satisfied that the Columbia River Fishing and Trading Company would prove a failure; nay, he was determined it should be so." McLoughlin put a rival fishery nearby and prevented the Chinook Indians from assisting Wyeth. "The Chinook," Bancroft said, "could take three fish out of the Columbia while the New Englanders took one out; but instead of assisting the Bostons of Wapato Island, the Chinooks opposed them." Not only were Wyeth's nets the wrong kind, but his men also quarreled with one another; some men were murdered, and eight of them drowned.[10]

Shortages of barrels and salt at times limited production. And even when fisheries were not confronted with competition for salmon or shortages

[3] Cicely Lyons, *Salmon: Our Heritage* (Vancouver: Mitchell Press Limited, 1969), pp. 140-141.

[4] *Pacific Fisherman* 29 (January 25, 1931), p. 85.

[5] Dictation of R. D. Hume, n.d. (Berkeley, Bancroft Library, University of California), p. 3.

[6] *Oregonian*, December 4, 1950, p. 18A.

[7] Manuscripts collection for people named (Portland, Oregon Historical Society); and Hubert H. Bancroft, *History of Oregon, Volume I, 1834-1848* (San Francisco: The History Company, 1886).

[8] Captain Spaulding, *Extracts from The Journal of Captain Spaulding of the Ship Lausanne, in the Year 1841,* (Washington, D.C., 1843) Third Session, Twenty-seventh Congress, Serial Set No. 426, p. 56.

[9] Philip Foster papers relating to Hawaii trade (Portland, Oregon Historical Society) MSS 996, Box 2.

[10] Bancroft, 1886, pp. 595-597 (see note 7).

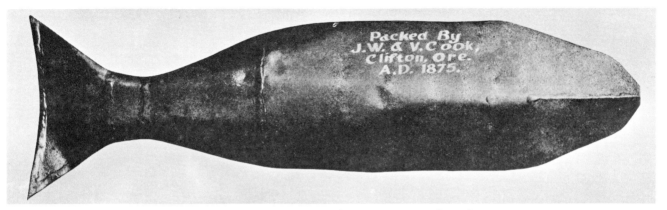

A Columbia River salmon canned and sealed in a tin made to fit (*Pacific Fisherman*, June 1929, p. 30).

of materials, they encountered shipping problems and unstable market conditions. During the early 1860s, oversupply caused the price to drop from $12 to $6 per barrel.[11]

A number of Columbia River salt salmon fisheries continued into the 1880s. In 1877 about 5,000 barrels were produced, which sold for $6 to $8 per barrel, with each cannery reportedly putting up 300 to 800 barrels.[12] However, soon after Hapgood, Hume and Company began operations on the Columbia in 1866, two salt salmon fisheries—John West and P. J. McGowan—also shifted to canning salmon. Others were soon to follow, and a new industry was spawned.

In 1866 Hapgood, Hume and Company packed and sold 4,000 cases of salmon for $16 per case. The company secured financial backing from broker William T. Coleman, and soon Hapgood and each of the Hume brothers had established his own canning operation on the Columbia. Later R. D. Hume and Isaac Smith bought out William Hume and Hapgood, and in 1870 they were joined by J. W. Cook. George Hume developed a partnership with Francis Cutting of San Francisco. The year 1871 brought new canning establishments. F. M. Warren opened at Cathlamet, and John West and Hodgkins located at Westport. Preserving salmon in cans proved to be an effective way to market the harvest. A can packed by John West in 1872 was purchased for 50 cents in 1888 by George Hume, who noted that "it was found to be [as] pure, sweet and palatable as when put up sixteen years ago."[13]

By 1873, seven canneries were in operation on the Columbia. George Hume and Hapgood, Hume and Company each had a cannery at Eagle Cliff; R. D. Hume was at Bay View; John Badollet was in Astoria; F. M. Warren, Sr., was at Cathlamet; and J. G. Megler and John West were at Brookfield and Westport.[14]

Canning salmon in 1873 was a simple process, requiring mostly hand labor. Charles Nordoff, traveler, described the process in a cannery he visited.

> The salmon are flung up on a stage, where they lie in heaps of a thousand at a time, a surprising sight to an Eastern person, for in such a pile you may see fish weighing from thirty to sixty pounds. The work of preparing them for the cans is conducted with exact method and great cleanliness, water being abundant. One Chinaman seizes a fish and cuts off his head; the next slashes off the fins and disembowels the fish; it then falls into a large vat, where the blood soaks out—a salmon bleeds like a bull—and after soaking and repeated washing in different vats, it falls at last into the hands of one of a gang of Chinese whose business it is, with heavy knives, to chop the fish into chunks of suitable size for the tins. These pieces are plunged into brine, and presently stuffed into the cans, it being

[11] Joseph A. Craig and Robert L. Hacker, "The History and Development of the Fisheries of the Columbia River," *Bulletin of the Bureau of Fisheries* 49 (1940), p. 150.

[12] Hubert H. Bancroft, *History of Washington, Idaho, and Montana, 1845-1889* (San Francisco: The History Company, 1890), p. 349.

[13] *Weekly Astorian*, April 7, 1888, p. 5.

[14] William H. Barker, "Reminiscences of the Salmon Industry," *Pacific Fisherman Yearbook* 18 (1920), p. 67; and Alfred A. Cleveland, "Social and Economic History of Astoria," *Oregon Historical Quarterly* 4 (June 1903), p. 140.

the object to fill each can as full as possible with fish, the bone being excluded. The top, which has a small hole pierced in it, is then soldered on, and five hundred tins set on a form are lowered into a huge kettle of boiling water, where they remain until the heat has expelled all the air. Then a Chinaman neatly drops a little solder over each pinhole, and after another boiling, the object of which is, I believe, to make sure that the cans are hermetically sealed, the process is complete.[15]

＊　＊　＊　＊

By 1875, according to R. D. Hume, "The canneries began to get numerous." There were 14 that year. "Up to 1879," Hume noted, "the business was fairly prosperous and there were no failures." George W. Hume was worth "half a million or more." William Hume was worth "about $400,-000."[16] Purchase price of a cannery with a 30,000-case capacity averaged $30,000. The largest item, 60 percent of the purchase price, was for the cannery and wharf. Boats for fishermen was the next largest expense, representing 20 percent of the cost. The twine for knitting nets was a yearly expense of about $5,000.[17]

As more and more canneries were built (there were 35 in 1880), the competition for fish and markets resulted in higher prices for fishermen and lower selling prices for the finished product. The pay to gillnetters increased from 15 cents per fish in 1866 to 50 cents by 1880. The price received per case of salmon decreased from $16 to $5.[18]

Cannerymen solved the problem of increased prices to fishermen and lower prices for the finished product by technical and organizational innovations. William H. Barker recounts how in the fall of 1876, J. G. Megler "visited the Centennial Exposition at Philadelphia and saw on exhibition the 'Howe' soldering machine." Megler wrote to

ROBERT D. HUME

JOSEPH HUME

[15] Charles Nordoff, "The Columbia River and Puget Sound," *Harper's Magazine* 49 (1974), p. 341.

[16] Hume, n.d., pp. 5-6 (see note 5).

[17] George Brown Goode and Associates, *The Fisheries and Fishery Industries of the United States* (Washington, D.C., 1887), Sec. V, Vol. 1, p. 746; and *Oregonian,* January 1, 1880.

[18] John S. Hittell, *The Commerce and Industries of the Pacific Coast of North America* (San Francisco: A. L. Bancroft & Co., 1882), p. 372.

GEORGE W. HUME

WILLIAM HUME

Pioneers of salmon canning industry on Columbia River (R. D. Hume photo, Oregon Historical Society; other photos, *Pacific Fisherman*, January 1920, pp. 73-74).

R. D. Hume describing how the machine soldered cans, and R. D. wired Megler to send him one.[19]

Each of the Hume brothers was noted for a particular innovative quality. R. D. introduced the Howe soldering machine, horse seining, the Halder seamer, and the double-bowed steam launch, and, with John West, made the first automatic can filler in 1882. R. D. was also the first to successfully operate a hatchery. He did this in 1877 when he moved from the Columbia to the Rogue River in southern Oregon. For years he fought an uphill battle to teach state and federal resource managers his hatchery methods. However, the most important of R. D. Hume's innovations was locating overseas markets. These included Australia, New Zealand, Latin America, the Far East, and, most significantly, England, where he demonstrated that salmon could provide cheap and nourishing food to workers in England's Midland industrial areas.[20]

George Hume was an innovator in business organization. Recognizing the need for capital, he secured a partnership with the wealthy Francis Cutting of San Francisco and opened a cannery at Astoria in 1875. He built two of the early canneries in Alaska and was one of the founders and a director of the Alaska Packers Association, which combined the canning interests in Alaska and reduced the salmon pack to make it more nearly compatible with the market potential. The Alaska Packers Association was used as a model in forming the Columbia River Packers Association and British Columbia Packers Association.

Joseph Hume was known for the quality of his product. His Star Brand was packed with only the largest salmon, caught within sight of his cannery. He said that he cooked them slowly since "too rapid cooling renders it strong, rancid, and unwholesome."[21] William Hume was known for being first to market each year, as reported in the April 11, 1879, *Weekly Astorian:* "Again, as usual, Mr.

[19] William H. Barker, 1920, p. 68 (see note 14).

[20] Gordon B. Dodds, *The Salmon King of Oregon, R. D. Hume and the Pacific Fisheries* (Chapel Hill: University of North Carolina Press, 1959), p. 6.

[21] Joseph Hume to F. H. Leggett & Co., April 7, 1879 (Portland, Oregon Historical Society), Scrapbook 13, p. 129.

Wm. Hume is first in the market with canned salmon this year."[22]

Other early canners, too, were innovators. Canneryman J. O. Hanthorn invented the rotary can washer in 1876. F. M. Warren, Sr., invented a retort for cooking salmon in 1877, which was widely used by canners along the coast. John West, who invented a can-filling machine with R. D. Hume, was among the first to find uses for cannery wastes. In 1873 he manufactured oil from wastes and by 1880 he was making fish meal.

One of the most important changes in the industry was in the location of canneries. Initially, they were located upriver. Eagle Cliff, the site of the Hapgood, Hume and Company cannery, was 50 miles from the mouth of the Columbia. John Badollet located the first cannery at Astoria in 1873. By 1880 over half of the Columbia River canneries were located there, only 17 miles from the Columbia River bar.

Innovators who were not canners also contributed to the inventiveness that maintained profits. Mathias Jensen, a Danish fisherman employed by the Astoria Iron Works, invented a machine that filled 48 cans per minute. John Fox, founder of the Astoria Iron Works, invented machines for making and soldering cans. Fox gained experience in the needs of the canned salmon industry by working for John West in 1873, R. D. Hume from 1881 to 1884, and George H. George in 1885.

The Hume family not only was a dominant force in the founding of the canned salmon industry, but also played an important part in its growth. Many of the men who were later important in the industry gained their experience working in or observing a Hume cannery. When Andrew Booth came to the Columbia, he was not allowed into any cannery to observe the canning process. Finally, R. D. Hume let Booth see his operation. Booth started a cannery in 1875. George H. George, who was vice president and general manager of the Columbia River Packers Association from 1910 to 1913, was bookkeeper for R. D. Hume and then went to work for Booth. Samuel Elmore learned salmon packing with Joseph Hume, and in 1881 he

bought him out. Elmore was one of the leaders in forming the Columbia River Packers Association in the 1890s. William H. Barker started with R. D. Hume in 1873, and in 1885 joined George H. George to form George and Barker, and later Eureka and Epicure, which merged into the Columbia River Packers Association. Barker, in 1904, became the general manager of the British Columbia Packers Association. His brother Fred, who had gained experience under Booth, became general manager of the Columbia River Packers Association in 1913.

The Humes, along with other Columbia River canners, were instrumental in spreading the idea of salmon canning to other areas. R. D. Hume left the Columbia in 1877 to establish his business on the Rogue River. William H. Barker said R. D. "seemed to think that the Columbia was getting fished out or soon would be."[23] Jackson and Meyers, who purchased R. D.'s Rainier cannery in 1874, opened a cannery on Puget Sound in 1877. Samuel Elmore developed canneries on five Oregon coastal streams. George and Joseph Hume opened canneries in Alaska. M. J. Kinney, who built a cannery in Astoria in 1876, opened an Alaska cannery in 1882 and started another there in 1883. B. A. Seaborg, owner of the Aberdeen Packing Company at Ilwaco, built a cannery in Alaska in 1887. Samuel Elmore and his partner George A. Sanborn opened an Alaska cannery in 1889. By 1896 Joseph Hume had moved his entire operation to Alaska. F. M. Warren, operator of two Columbia River canneries, named his company Portland and Alaska Packing Company, emphasizing his Alaska interests; thus, the canning of salmon was spread by a relatively small core of men, many of whom gained their initial canning experience in association with one of the Hume brothers.

❖   ❖   ❖   ❖

Between 1866 and 1884, the Columbia River salmon pack experienced steady growth, reaching a peak in 1883 and 1884. During each of these years more than 600,000 cases of salmon were

---

[22] *Weekly Astorian*, April 11, 1879.

[23] Barker, 1920, p. 68 (see note 14).

packed, representing two-thirds of the entire Pacific Coast pack. However, this remarkable growth was followed by a decline. By 1889, only 310,000 cases were packed.[24]

Prior to the decline, profits were good. For 1879 R. D. Hume noted that "those who had been in the business before that time made money, but I do not believe that any money has been made since."[25] The *Oregonian* of January 1, 1882, reported on the change in the attitudes of cannerymen toward profits by saying "Cannerymen have learned to content themselves with fair returns such as any other regular business would pay, while in former days a fortune was expected and made each season." After the decline the season's report in the *Weekly Astorian* stated, "The close of the salmon season of 1887 is as financially unsatisfactory to many of the canners as the close of preceding years."[26] The claim was that middlemen and wholesalers were making all the profits. John Badollet was quoted as saying, "The time for high profits for the majority of establishments has passed." Badollet continued, "There is so much competition, that the catch is much less for the boat on an average, the supply of fish is not constant, and the cost of the cannery has doubled without any corresponding increase in the price of the canned product." Since the season lasts only three months, "its brevity gives the men employed to fish and can, excellent opportunities for striking, for they know that it is a difficult matter to get others in their places without a serious loss of production."[27]

The success of canned salmon attracted cannerymen and fishermen to the Columbia. New entrants competed with those already there for fish and markets. Canning salmon and locating markets for the product increased the pressure on the Columbia River's salmon resource. Since the resource was limited, each new canner took a portion of the pack available to other canners. And each new fisherman took a portion of the catch that could have been made by other fishermen. Too many canners and fishermen competed for too few fish.

However, even if the declining salmon resources had not limited this expansion, the limits of the market would have had the same effect. Cannerymen knew in 1883-1884 that they had saturated the market. They tried, but failed, to limit production. They failed to reach agreement because each canner wanted to maintain or improve his competitive position. Established canners wanted a production limit based on cannery capacity, while newcomers wanted the boats divided evenly to each cannery. The key to success in this situation was inventiveness. Inventiveness determined whether or not a canner stayed in business.

The combination of a limited salmon resource and a saturated market caused reduction of the salmon pack after 1884. The market constraint was eased somewhat when 10 percent of the 1884 pack was lost at sea. The innovators, however, were taking fish formerly caught by the less innovative. In addition, the more successful operators sought to expand by hiring the best fishermen and capturing a larger share of the consumer market.

Table 1. Columbia River Salmon Pack, by Cannery, 1880-1889

Year	Total pack (cases)	No. canneries	Avg. pack (cases)
1880	539,600	29	18,600
1881	549,000	34	16,100
1882	540,800	35	15,500
1883	634,300	40	15,900
1884[a]	571,200	35	16,800
1885	543,300	35	15,500
1886[b]	435,100	40	10,900
1887[c]	354,000	38	9,300
1888	362,300	27	13,400
1889	323,000	24	13,500

Source: George Brown Goode and Associates, *The Fisheries and Fishery Industries of the United States* (Washington, D.C., 1887), Sec. V, Vol. 1, p. 751; John S. Hittell, *The Commerce and Industries of the Pacific Coast of North America* (San Francisco: A. L. Bancroft & Co., 1882), p. 380; and January 1 issues of the *Oregonian*, 1883-1887, and August 9 issues of the *Oregonian*, 1887 and 1890.

[a] Cases not standardized for 48-pound cases. There are variances with standardized figures.

[b] Number of cases shipped; all other years, number of cases packed.

[c] Pack through August; all other years, full-year totals.

[24] *Pacific Fisherman* 29 (January 25, 1931), p. 85.
[25] Hume, n.d., p. 5 (see note 5).
[26] *Weekly Astorian*, August 20, 1887.
[27] Goode, 1887, p. 739 (see note 17).

Data for 1880-1889 show the distribution of pack among cannerymen. Table 1 gives the total and average pack for each of these years. It shows the growth and decline cycle in the total pack and in the average pack per cannery. From 1884 to 1887, the average pack declined from 16,800 to 9,300 cases per cannery. During this period the number of canneries remained high, at 35 to 40. The number of canneries declined to 24 in 1888-1889. Some canneries went out of business; several cannerymen "combined in pairs, with the result of greatly economizing on the cost of canning."[28] The canners with sufficient capital, good fishing conditions, new canning technology, and satisfactory markets remained in business.

Table 2 illustrates this point. It ranks the top canneries based on the ratio of their pack to the average annual pack for all canneries for the 1880-1889 period. Note the names of "the innovators."

Table 2.   Columbia River Canners with Highest Productivity, 1880-1889

Company (Top 16 of 69)	Ratio Company pack/ average pack
F. M. Warren (2 canneries)	2.2
George & Barker (2 canneries)	2.1
M. J. Kinney	2.0
A. Booth & Sons	1.5
J. Badollet & Co.	1.4
J. W. & V. Cook	1.4
Columbia Canning Co.	1.4
John A. Devlin	1.3
William Hume (2 canneries)	1.3
J. G. Megler	1.3
Francis Cutting	1.2
J. O. Hanthorn	1.2
Joseph Hume	1.2
B. A. Seaborg	1.2
George W. Hume	1.1
Scandinavian Packing Co.	1.1

SOURCE: Same as in Table 1.

[28] *Oregonian*, January 1, 1887.

Chapter 4/

Immigrant Laborers

SETTLEMENT OF the Columbia River basin and the introduction of salmon canning had a marked effect on salmon resources once harvested almost exclusively by Native Americans. Indians continued to fish dipnets in their traditional fishing grounds, but their catches were rapidly diminishing. Gillnetters, trapmen, seiners, fishwheelers, purse seiners, and trollers all competed for a share of the catch as canned salmon became an increasingly important part of the world's food supply. Overall, gillnetters were the most numerous and best organized, and through the mid-1930s they harvested the biggest share of the salmon resource.

The salmon fishery was a source of jobs for immigrants to the United States. Occidental immigrants from Europe became fishers and Oriental immigrants worked in the canneries. Initially, these immigrants were sought as an inexpensive labor force, but later they were excluded for not being citizens.

*　*　*　*

The Clatsop County census of 1880 provides the first indication of the ethnic contribution to the salmon canning industry. The census was taken in June, during the peak of the salmon canning season, and 15 salmon canneries were operating within the county.

The census counted 7,055 people in Clatsop County, including 2,045 Chinese, the largest single ethnic group. Eighty percent of the Chinese

worked in the salmon canneries. The remainder were laborers, cooks, washermen, tailors, grocers, barbers, physicians, gardeners, pawnbrokers, a butcher, and a baker.

Chinese were first employed as cannery laborers by George W. Hume in 1872. White laborers who had been used previously proved to be too transient and unreliable. The Chinese were fast workers; some could clean a 40-pound salmon in 45 seconds. A man skilled with the knife could clean 1,700 fish in an 11-hour day. A Chinese laborer was said to have "the strength of a man in his hands, and his hands were as nimble as a woman's."[1]

An 1888 government study indicated that the average Chinese laborer made $180 to $200 during the cannery season, an average of $40 to $50 per month.[2] The Columbia River Fishermen's Protective Union estimated the average gillnetter made $45 per month for the 1888 season.[3]

Cannery work, as fishing, was a seasonal activity. In the off-season the Chinese laborers who came to the Columbia from Portland, San Fran-

[1] Francis Seufert, *A Short History of Seufert Brothers Company, Salmon Packers at The Dalles, Oregon, 1881-1954* (Portland, Oregon Historical Society, 1958), MSS 1102, p. 14.
[2] J. W. Collins, "Report of the Fisheries of the Pacific Coast of the United States," *Report of the Commissioner of Fish and Fisheries for 1888* (Washington, D.C., 1892), p. 207.
[3] Columbia River Fishermen's Protective Union, Pamphlet (Astoria, 1890), p. 14.

23

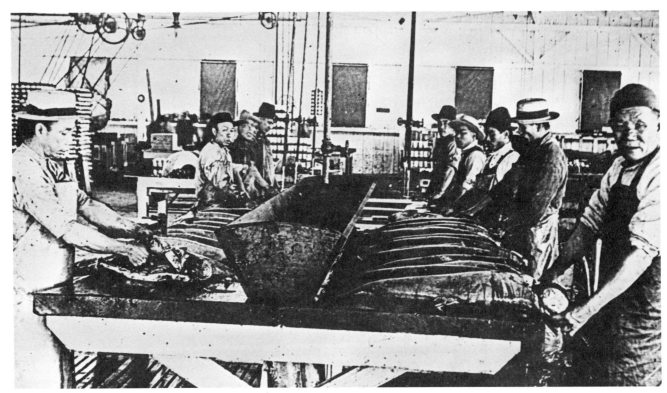

Chinese cutting salmon (Douglas County Historical Society).

cisco, and Seattle returned to these cities to work as laborers in agriculture, lumber, railroad repair, construction, and in service and other odd jobs.

By the 1890s the contract labor system was established. This involved an agreement between a cannery and a Chinese contractor who provided laborers and assumed responsibility for recruiting, hiring, feeding, and paying them. A Chinese crew coming to the Columbia would not start work on a Friday, believing that to do so would be bad luck. The Chinese cleaned, packed, cooked, labeled, and boxed the salmon. Nearly all cannery labor, with the exception of some white supervisory personnel, was contract labor.

The contract labor system was an exploitation of laborers by both the canners and the Chinese contractor. Wages were low and food was poor, consisting of boiled rice, seaweed, and tea. The contractor sold clothing and other items to workers at exorbitant prices, and added to his profit by assuming the role of the "house" in gambling activities among the crew. Chinese workers were characterized as "inveterate gamblers, and their

wages, as earned, go from one to another to pay their gaming debts."[4] Drug abuse was another characteristic of the contract labor system. Drugs were used both to lure and control workers.

Investigations by the National Recovery Administration during the depression of the 1930s exposed the abuses of the contract labor system. By this time Chinese laborers were being replaced by Japanese, Mexican, Filipino, and women laborers. The system was further weakened by the establishment of strong cannery unions during the depression. However, Chinese crews were used as late as 1953 in Columbia River canneries.

Increasing competition in the marketplace soon forced canners to take a closer look at the efficiency of their operations. Historically, manufacturing efficiency has been improved by replacing manual labor with machines. By the early 1900s, Chinese workers who cleaned salmon were giving way to a machine called the "Iron Chink." The Iron Chink

[4] George Brown Goode and Associates, *The Fisheries and Fishery Industries of The United States* (Washington, D.C., 1887), Sec. IV, p. 42.

Woman cannery worker (from John N. Cobb's glass slides, University of Washington).

was not the only machine substituting for manual labor in the salmon canneries. It was, however, an extraordinary example of this process.

Development of the Iron Chink began in Seattle about 1901. The principal inventor, E. A. Smith, tested his invention at the Bellingham, Washington, plant of the United Fishing and Packing Company in 1903. Production and sales to canneries began in 1905, when the first model was sold to Pacific American Fisheries. The Iron Chink could prepare salmon for packing at the rate of 45 per minute.[5] One machine thus could do the work of 30 to 40 Chinese laborers. The cutting knives were self-adjusting and self-sharpening. Salmon of any size weighing from 1 to 50 pounds could be cleaned, although the machine operated most efficiently when fish were of fairly uniform size. By 1918, the Model G could butcher and slime up to 60 salmon per minute.[6]

The Iron Chink, along with the sanitary tin can, vastly increased the efficiency of salmon canners. Although the machine replaced many Chinese workers, the Chinese Exclusion Act created enough of a labor shortage that few laborers in the crews were displaced. Chinese crews continued to work in the canneries, later being replaced by other immigrant groups.

❋   ❋   ❋   ❋

While Oriental immigrants provided the main labor source for the canneries, Occidental immigrants were recruited for fishing. A major exception to this was on the Fraser River in British Columbia, where half of the fishermen were Japanese prior to World War I. Japanese entered the Fraser River salmon fishery because "white men willing to engage in gill net fishing were few in numbers, and the fishing was done chiefly by Japanese and Indians."[7] In northern British Columbia and Alaska, Native Americans were recruited to fish, but often this was done mainly to attract native women for employment in the canneries.

On the Columbia River the Occidental-fisher and Oriental-cannery division of labor was strictly maintained. When Chinese cannery workers tried to fish, they were swiftly dissuaded. The September 21, 1880, *San Francisco Chronicle* reported that the Chinese "never venture on the river, for the fishermen are not the class to tamely submit to such competition. Some years ago a few adventurous Mongolians joined the fleet, but they disappeared the same night. Their boats were broken to pieces, and their nets cut up and scattered on the beach. The fishermen made no attempt to conceal the fact that they had drowned the intruders."

G. B. Goode estimated there were 2,500 fishermen on the Columbia River in 1880.[8] The Clatsop County census provided general statistics on more than half of this total. Of the 1,293 Clatsop County fishermen, 91 percent were single. Most, 86 percent, were boarders at local rooming houses. They came to the Columbia for the fishing season, with most of them originating from San Francisco.

[5] *Pacific Fisherman Yearbook* 25 (1927), pp. 112-113.
[6] *Pacific Fisherman* 1 (January 20, 1903), p. 13; and vol. 16 (September 1918), p. 39.

[7] *Report of Special Fishery Commission, 1917* (Ottawa, 1918), p. 30.
[8] George Brown Goode, 1887, p. 42 (see note 4).

Feeding the "Iron Chink" (Oregon Historical Society).

When asked their place of birth, only 13 percent gave the United States. Only 16, or 1 percent, were born in Oregon. Scandinavia was the most often mentioned place of birth, with 44 percent of the fishermen indicating they were born there. A total of 224 fishermen listed Sweden as their place of birth. Norway, Finland, and Denmark followed with 142, 140, and 49, respectively. Assuming that the 42 listing Russia as their homeland were Finns (Finland was at that time part of Russia), the Finns would be the second most numerous group. Of the six in every seven who were foreign-born, 95 percent were from Europe.[9]

The ethnicity of fishers correlated with the gear they used. Each immigrant group used the type of gear most closely associated with its ethnic background. Gillnetters and trapmen were primarily Scandinavians. Dipnets continued to be used mainly by the Indians. Purse seines were introduced to the Columbia by Austrians. Trollers were more likely to be from western Europe. The crews who operated the horse seines were usually ethnically or socially homogeneous. For example, there were crews composed of Danes, Swedes, Norwegians, and college students.

Seven major groups of commercial fishers competed with one another for the Columbia River salmon catch. Most numerous were gillnetters. Others were trapmen, seiners, fishwheelers, dipnetters, purse seiners, and trollers, the latter group becoming more important during World War I. In addition to ethnicity and gear type, the fishers sorted themselves into groups according to community.

The first gillnet on the Columbia River was reported to have come from Bath, Maine, and was fished by a man named Hodgkins in 1853.[10] Hapgood, Hume and Company used two gillnets and four fishermen to put up their first salmon pack on the Columbia River. The two boats harvested more than one-quarter million pounds of salmon. When gillnetters became numerous, the average catch was 10,000 pounds per season. Gillnetters were always the most numerous group of fishermen employed. A peak of 2,800 gillnets was reached about 1915 (see Appendix A). Gillnets also were the most versatile type of equipment. They could be fished in high and low water when the river was muddy or clear. Typically, they were fished at night, with the gillnetter resting during the day. Gillnets were used from the bar to Celilo Falls, 200 miles upstream. They were most numerous on the lower Columbia, with most gillnetters living or boarding in Astoria. As a group, gillnetters sought to dominate the river.

Salmon fishing on the Columbia, 1880s (Cleveland Rockwell painting, *Harper's New Monthly Magazine*, December 1882, p. 12).

Gillnetters organized the Columbia River Fishermen's Protective Union in the late 1880s for the purpose of advancing their interests. Fishermen's organizations were reported as early as 1875.[11] The *Daily Astorian* carried a notice on May 23, 1876, requesting "any fishermen on the Columbia River, wishing to join the Fishermen's Association" to apply to Thomas Dealey, its secretary. At the June 17 meeting, the members adopted regulations for governing the Columbia River Fishermen's Benefit Aid Society and listed eight drifting grounds they wished to be recognized.[12]

Either there were several organizations or the 1876 one was unsuccessful. The May 16, 1879, *Daily Astorian* carried a notice to all fishermen

[9] U.S. Census Office, *Tenth Census, June 1, 1880* (Washington, D.C., 1883-1884), microfilm.

[10] Joseph A. Craig and Robert L. Hacker, "The History and Development of the Fisheries of the Columbia River," *Bulletin of the Bureau of Fisheries* 49 (1940), p. 165.

[11] Fred Andrus, "CRFPU Older Than Thought," *Daily Astorian*, January 9, 1975, p. 4.

[12] *Daily Astorian*, June 1, 1876, p. 2.

"who are interested in their welfare are requested to attend a meeting . . . for the purpose of organizing a Fishermen's Protective Union." The union was organized May 24, 1879, and members marched in the Astoria Fourth of July parade that year.[13] However, the union was weakened by apathy and intimidation. On April 24, 1880, a meeting to settle on a fish price was interrupted by a bomb which dispersed the crowd. A fisherman, O. V. Carter, declared that "they were too few to maintain the strike."[14]

A Columbia River Fishermen's Protective Union was formed again in Astoria on April 11, 1886, and the union soon forced the canneries to increase the price offered per fish from 55 to 65 cents. According to the union pamphlet the canners "learned to fear and respect the power of the laboring men when they stand united, and the fishermen had learned that their only hope to better their condition lay in banding together and enforcing their rights through organized effort."[15] The union was a formidable force. By 1888 canneries were paying $1.25 per fish. Key to the union's strength were the committeemen who solicited and maintained high levels of membership at each cannery. Committeemen were paid $50 per month during the fishing season. Dues included a $5 initiation fee and a monthly contribution of $1 during the fishing season. The union had amassed $11,055.86 on deposit at Y. W. Case's by August 25, 1888.[16] The union president, secretary, and treasurer were each paid $75 a month for overseeing the union's interests. Among these activities were attempts to secure removal of traps from Baker Bay and from the best drifting grounds on the Washington side near the Columbia River bar. To accomplish this, the union petitioned the U.S. Army Corps of Engineers and sent a lobbyist to the State Legislature. Union resources were used to organize fishermen on other rivers and harbors in Oregon and Washington.

The union maintained a reading room and hired a detective to reduce the problem of net thefts. Lights were maintained on Sand Island as aids to navigation. Gillnetting was a hazardous occupation and many fishermen died each year. The union paid widows a small sum, typically $45, to aid with burial costs of deceased members. Storms were a constant danger to the fishermen. Since the best fishing was close to the Columbia River bar, boats frequently were carried across the bar with no possibility of return, and many fishermen died at sea from exposure. More than 20 men died in a sudden storm that came up on the night of May 3, 1880. Because a strike had just been settled, there were large numbers of fishermen on the river. When the storm struck, many were swept across the bar and lost. Mr. Acklan reported in the *Daily Astorian* seeing two men clinging to the bottom of their gillnet boat heading for the breakers. He said that he could do nothing to save the men, and "they bid farewell by tipping their hats as they entered the jaws of death."[17]

In the 1880s, 20 to 60 fishermen were estimated to die each year. The *San Francisco Chronicle* of September 21, 1880, reported estimates as high as 250 fatalities per year. A government report indicated that 54 men died during the 1893 season.[18]

The union was interested in the activities of canners and businessmen, too. To maintain the quality image of Columbia River canned salmon, in 1896 they demanded a stop to packing Puget Sound "dog" salmon (chum salmon) as Columbia River spring chinook. To support unionism in general, members were asked in 1890 to boycott Weinhard's Brewery. Union members were asked "to do their best in the matter as it was a case of unionism against capital."[19]

Union activities were carefully guarded. Meetings were held in secret and were often long. The April 15, 1887, meeting lasted from 1 p.m. to 10 p.m. Union membership was severely restricted.

[13] *Daily Astorian*, July 6, 1879, p. 3.

[14] *Oregonian*, April 24, 1880, p. 1.

[15] Columbia River Fishermen's Protective Union, 1890, p. 14 (see note 3).

[16] Columbia River Fishermen's Protective Union, Central Board Meeting (Portland, Oregon Historical Society), MSS 70 (microfilm).

[17] *Daily Astorian*, May 6, 1880, p. 3.

[18] Hugh M. Smith, "Notes on a Reconnaissance of the Fisheries of the Pacific Coast of the United States in 1894," *Bulletin of the Fish Commission* 14 (1895), p. 237.

[19] Columbia River Fishermen's Protective Union, Minutes (Portland, Oregon Historical Society) MSS 70, October 7, 1890 (microfilm).

Columbia River salmon trap (Gifford and Prentiss photo, Oregon Historical Society).

The constitution read: "No liquor dealer, gambler, politician, capitalist, lawyer, agent for capitalists, nor persons holding office, whether under national, state or municipal government shall under any consideration become members."[20] Because of the ethnic backgrounds of members, Finnish was often spoken at meetings. Union members used a password to identify themselves and painted their boats with a special insignia. Meetings were often boisterous, and union members disturbing order were removed by the sergeant at arms.

The Columbia River Fishermen's Protective Union remained strong until the strike of 1896. During this strike, which was probably the most bitter ever on the Columbia River, the canners

organized to maintain stronger bargaining power in the face of union demands. The strike lasted for nearly three months and included violence in which at least one man was killed. The National Guards of Oregon and Washington were called out to maintain order. Businesses that depended upon fishermen for their earnings were hard hit. The union snag puller, the schooner *Pathfinder*, was used to pull traps in the vicinity of Sand Island. This was done to intimidate trapmen and prevent them from fishing during the strike. In retaliation, canners considered bringing strikebreakers from the Atlantic Coast.

On June 21 the union accepted the canners' compromise offer of 4½ cents per pound, with both sides claiming victory. The losers, it turned out, were the fishermen. Canners had learned the value

[20] Collins, 1892, p. 205 (see note 2).

of banding together. They continued to use this tactic successfully, holding fish prices to 6 cents per pound or less through 1917. In 1917, demand stimulated by World War I increased the price paid for fish to 10 cents per pound.

Cooperation among canners did more than stabilize fish prices. Canners also were able to save on other costs. In 1913, George H. George, general manager of the Columbia River Packers Association, obtained an agreement among canners "that there should not be any bonus given away to fishermen, also that each packer would respect and not try to hire men formerly fishing for his competitors."[21] This saved canners an estimated ½ cent per pound.

In 1917 the fishermen's union dissolved, and the Columbia River Fishermen's League was organized in 1918. In 1921 the league negotiated a 9 cents per pound price for fish for its 1,500 members, with the canners agreeing to absorb the new poundage tax and to reduce the cost of twine from $4 to $3 per pound. Since "the average fisherman uses about four papers of twine a year with 24 pounds to the paper, it gives a saving of $86.40."[22] Fishermen were apathetic because 1921 was a depression year in the salmon market. The league passed out of existence.

Carl Pruitt, who had organized the league, reorganized the Columbia River Fishermen's Protective Union in 1926. The canners offered a price of 10 cents per pound for fish. Fishermen struck for 15 cents, then settled for 13½ cents. By 1930 the union had 600 to 700 members and had secured a price increase to 17 cents per pound, but membership declined with the onset of the depression. In 1932, membership dwindled to 200 and the fish price dropped to 6 cents per pound. The union expanded to include cannery workers in 1933 and again went on strike for higher fish prices. The settlement of 8 cents per pound revived the union. Membership totaled 1,500 fishermen and 900 cannery workers. After 1933 union membership continued to grow and decline sporadically with economic conditions in the fishery.

The pound nets of trapmen competed most directly with the gillnetters. A modern commercial pound net was constructed in Baker Bay, across the Columbia from Astoria, by O. P. Graham in 1879. The north side of the Columbia continued to be the primary site for pound nets until they were eliminated by a Washington state initiative petition in 1934.

Salmon, as they entered the river, followed a course along the north shore, passing through Baker Bay. The Columbia River Fishermen's Protective Union stated about pound nets: "The reason why our gillnet fishermen were compelled to fish at or on the bar, and brave the dangers of the breakers at the mouth of the Columbia River, was mainly owing to the fish traps taking up all the best fishing grounds, and left to a fisherman with a gill-net no space over which to float or drift his net, and it is, alas too true, that many were caught in the breakers and drowned."[23]

In 1890 there were 168 traps. The next year the number increased to 238. More than 400 were fished in 1927, the peak year on record (Appendix A). Competition from the traps was overcome by two gillnetters. The September 1908 *Pacific Fisherman* reported that two gillnetters were discovered fishing in a trap. "They were waiting for the fish in the pot to get gilled in their net."[24]

Pound nets were constructed each year by driving piles and hanging a net to catch salmon. The salmon were led successively through the leads, heart, pot, and spiller of the trap. The concept was to take advantage of the salmon's natural desire to always swim upstream.

Trapmen argued the advantages of their gear over gillnets. The principal advantage was the ability to limit the catch to match canning capacity. Quality of the canned salmon improved because fish could be packed within a few hours after taken from the water.

During the mid-1880s canneries established limits on the amount of salmon that could be landed. Limits were typically set at 30 fish per day. Trapmen argued that because of these limits gill-

[21] Fred Barker to A. B. Hammond, October 31, 1913 (Portland, Oregon Historical Society) MSS 1699, Box 22.
[22] *Morning Astorian*, May 10, 1921.

[23] Columbia River Fishermen's Protective Union, 1890, p. 8 (see note 3).
[24] *Pacific Fisherman* 6 (September 1908), p. 26.

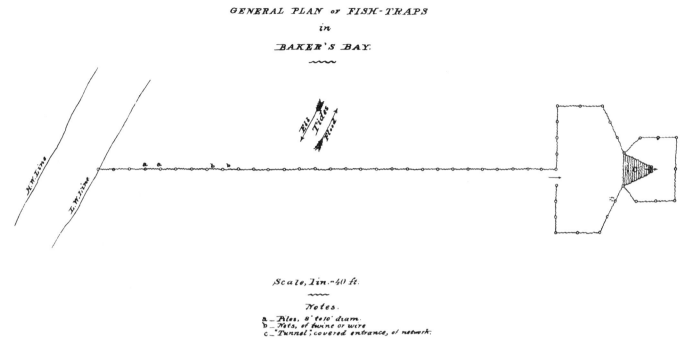

General plan of fish traps in Baker Bay, 1887 (W. A. Jones, *The Salmon Fisheries of the Columbia River*, Senate Document 123, Serial Set No. 2510).

netters wasted large quantities of fish by throwing their excess catch overboard. The trapman, on the other hand, "went out to his net and would estimate one hundred salmon swimming about in the pound. He placed thirty in his boat for delivery, and seeing enough fish in the pound for the next two or three days, he closed the tunnel to the net."[25]

The average pound net of the 1880s could be constructed for $800. Those employed in fishing the pound nets earned an average of $65 per month.[26] Most of the trapmen were Washington state citizens who farmed as well as fished.

* * * *

Gillnets and traps were gear fished primarily by individuals. Initially, gillnets were owned by the canneries and rented to fishermen, but a system was arranged in 1888 whereby a fisherman could purchase the gear and pay for it with a portion of the receipts for his catch. Canners also owned some of the trap sites, but most sites were developed by individuals. This was a unique feature of the Columbia River fishery. In most other salmon fisheries, particularly Puget Sound and Alaska, trap sites were owned and fished by the canners. Fishermen in these areas considered this system to be a device by which the canners could circumvent the need for their labors and obtain fish at a lower price. On the Columbia, however, trapmen sold their fish under the same arrangements as gillnetters. Trapmen often were accused by gillnetters of not supporting their fish price, but both groups were independent of direct control by the canneries.

Seines and fishwheels were the gear canners used to compete with the individual gillnetters and trapmen. Seines were fished on the Columbia's sandy shoals, competing with gillnetters and trapmen for fish and, in some instances, for fishing locations.

Small beach seines were used by Indians and early settlers. In 1895 R. D. Hume refined this technique by using horses to haul the seines. At that time 84 seines were in use. During the peak years of 1927 and 1928, the number increased to 100.

[25] Washington Fishermen's Association, *Washington Salmon Fisheries on the Columbia* (Ilwaco, circa 1893), p. 8.

[26] Washington Fishermen's Association, 1893, pp. 10-12 (see note 25).

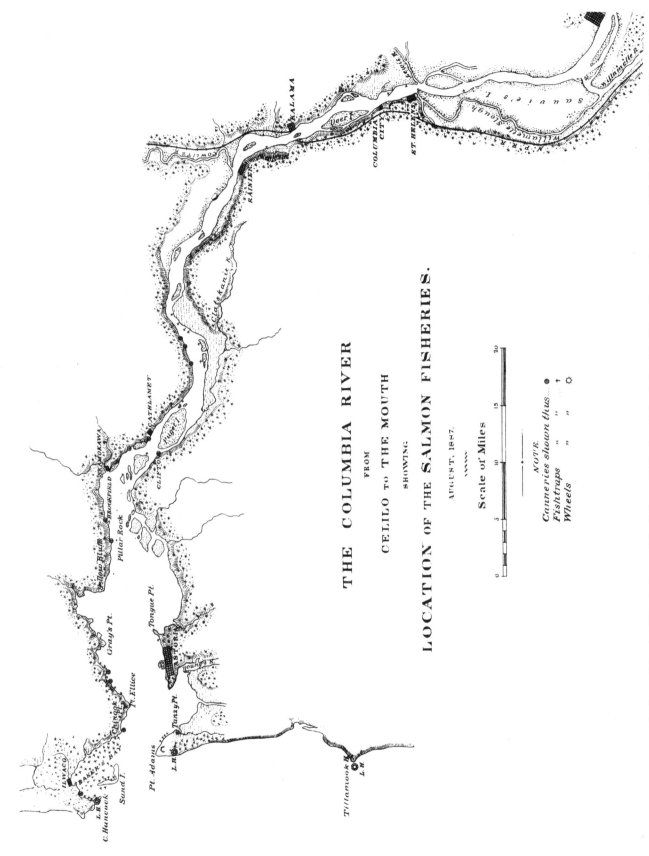

Location of salmon fisheries (W. A. Jones, *The Salmon Fisheries of the Columbia River*, Senate Document 123, Serial Set No. 2510).

Seine crews varied in size. The typical company crew included 20 to 40 men and 5 to 7 teams of horses. Individuals also operated small seines, but their take was small. The best seining grounds were located at three sites on Sand Island near the mouth of the Columbia. In 1905 the U.S. government laid out seining sites and rented them to the highest bidder. In 1908 the Columbia River Packers Association successfully bid on sites 2 and 3, and in 1911 they obtained all three sites, which they held through 1918. The annual rent for the three sites was $14,154 in the 1916-1918 period.[27]

sundown. Ernest Woodfield was the Sand Island seine foreman for the Columbia River Packers Association. On July 31, 1912, his Sand Island seine took 20,000 pounds—10,000 pounds in one haul.[28] A record day was August 22, 1921, when 60,000 pounds were caught in one haul. The crews fishing that day obtained a total catch of 188,000 pounds.[29] Upstream near Celilo Falls, the Seufert Brothers Company also operated several seines. One seine harvested 70,000 pounds on September 13, 1947, just two years before seines were outlawed by Oregon voters.[30]

Seining for salmon on the Columbia River (Ernest Woodfield photo, Columbia River Maritime Museum).

Seine-caught salmon were cheaper for the canneries. The seine foreman was paid a basic wage plus shares of the total landings as an incentive to catch more fish. Seiners received $1.75 per day in 1912; by 1916 their wages had increased to $2.50 per day. Sometimes there was a bonus for staying the whole season.

Seines were most effective when the river was low. Catches were usually heaviest at daybreak and poorest in the early afternoon, but hauls were made regularly throughout the day from sunup to

The fishwheel, a device operated by the river's current, required fast water upriver. It competed with dipnets for fishing locations. Some gillnets and seines also were used on the upper river, but they competed with the dipnets only for fish and not for fishing sites. The primary fishwheel and dipnet sites were at the Cascades of the Columbia and Celilo Falls. Each of these areas now has been covered by water behind mainstream dams. Bonne-

[27] Major Henry C. Jewett to Columbia River Packers Association, April 26, 1916 (Portland, Oregon Historical Society), MSS 1699, Box 51.

[28] Notation on photograph in collections of Columbia River Maritime Museum, Astoria.

[29] Notation on photograph in collections of Columbia River Maritime Museum, Astoria.

[30] Seufert, 1958, p. 29 (see note 1).

Columbia River salmon caught in a seine on Sand Island (Ernest Woodfield photo, University of Washington).

Stationary fishwheel with recreation angler fishing in lead, 1887 (W. A. Jones, *The Salmon Fisheries of the Columbia River*, Senate Document 123, Serial Set No. 2510).

Scow wheel at the head of Cascade Rapids on the Washington side of the Columbia River (Oregon Historical Society).

ville Dam was completed at the Cascades in 1938, and the reservoir behind The Dalles Dam covered Celilo Falls in 1957.

Fishwheels had been used in the Carolinas as early as 1829, but the first fishwheel on the Columbia was erected in 1879 by Samuel Wilson. The maximum number used on the Columbia was in about 1899, when 76 were in operation.[31] Fishwheels caught large numbers of bluebacks. Because of declining blueback runs after 1900, the number of wheels dropped to 50 by 1909. In 1934, the last year fishwheels could operate after being eliminated by a Washington state initiative petition, there were only 27.

[31] Ivan J. Donaldson and Frederick K. Cramer, *Fishwheels of the Columbia* (Portland: Binfords & Mort, 1971), p. 1.

Only one man was required to tend a fishwheel, and the wheel caught large quantities of salmon at costs lower than the prices paid to gillnetters or trapmen. Fishwheels were of two types, stationary and scow wheels. Scow wheels were used on barges and, because of their mobility, could be moved to the best fishing sites as determined by river stages. Stationary wheels usually were constructed at consistently good fishing sites.

Most fishwheels were erected by canners. Two families, the Warrens and the Seuferts, owned a third of the wheels. The Warrens operated a cannery on the Oregon side of the Columbia at the Cascades, and the Seufert's cannery was near Celilo Falls. Of the 79 stationary wheels known to have operated on the upper Columbia, the Warren family owned 10 and the Seuferts owned 19. The two families also owned 6 and 17 scow wheels, respectively.[32]

The most famous fishwheel was Seufert's No. 5. Constructed in 1887 at a cost of $8,890.97, it was operated through 1926 when fishwheels on the Oregon side of the river were eliminated by initiative petition. No. 5 averaged 146,000 pounds of salmon per year. Its best year was 1906, with a catch of 418,000 pounds. The largest single-day catch for No. 5 was on May 10, 1913, when it captured 70,000 pounds. The poorest year was 1926, when only 21,000 pounds were caught.[33] One of the least effective fishwheels was the Klindt wheel, erected in 1896. For 20 years the Klindts walked a mile each day to the wheel to remove, at most, two or three salmon. Walter Klindt noted that the problem with the wheel was "the fish runs were

FRANK M. WARREN, SR.

diminishing and the fish remaining had too much room to go by."[34]

Catch data are available for 13 Warren wheels —10 stationary and 3 scow—for 1920 and 1921. These data indicate very little difference between the catch for stationary and scow wheels. The 13 wheels averaged 19,500 pounds each for 1920 and 28,000 pounds each for 1921. While the average fishwheel catch increased 50 percent, the total Columbia River poundage caught in 1920-1921 decreased by 25 percent, as total catch dropped from 36 to 27 million pounds. The recorded catch of the wheels varied from day to day and year to year. During 1920 and 1921, the Wheel No. 1 catch increased from 25,000 to 75,000 pounds; for Wheel No. 20, the catch dropped from 13,000 to 700 pounds. Daily catches ranged from 0 to more than 100 salmon. Daily counts tended to reflect the runs of fish, which peaked at Wheel No. 1 around July 7, 1920. The 1921 peak was earlier, on June 21, and four times greater.[35]

FRANCIS A. SEUFERT

[32] Frank M. Warren papers (Portland, Oregon Historical Society), Ledger Vol. 14, MSS 1141; and Seufert, 1958, p. 6 (see note 1).

[33] Donaldson and Cramer, 1971, p. 91 (see note 31).

[34] Donaldson and Cramer, 1971, p. 99 (see note 31).

[35] Warren Papers, Ledger Vol. 14 (see note 32).

Puget Sound purse seiners operated on the Columbia River for a brief period (Asahel Curtis photo, Washington State Historical Society).

For a brief period purse seines were introduced on the Columbia. The purse seine had been used on Puget Sound since the 1890s. William Graham of Ilwaco, Washington, began using this gear on the Columbia in 1905, and it was used intensively during World War I when Austrian fishermen from Puget Sound started fishing the lower Columbia. Purse seiners competed directly with gillnetters for fishing areas. A 1918 Columbia River Packers Association memo cautioned each purse seiner not to "throw out his net, so that when he purses his net, it will take in the gillnetter's net."[36]

The impact of Puget Sound purse seiners was significant in 1917. Catch data are lacking, but purse seines made a significant social impact. Because they were fished predominantly by Austrians at the time of World War I, one gillnetter summed

[36] Fred Barker to J. V. Giaconi, July 25, 1918 (Portland, Oregon Historical Society), MSS 1699, Box 50.

up his frustrations to U.S. Food Administrator, Herbert Hoover, by writing, "Now the Austrian enemies are allowed to be here on the river, and not only take the fish belonging to us, but destroying our nets besides."[37] On the side of the purse seiners, J. G. Megler, a canner, wrote Hoover, "This is a free country. We do not believe that any man should be restricted from work and let the greater number throw him out of work in a legitimate business because he is in the minority."[38]

The quantity of fish taken by the purse seiners and their competition with gillnetters, who were the dominant force on the Columbia, soon led to legislation for their exclusion. By 1922 the legislatures of Oregon and Washington enacted laws to exclude purse seines from the Columbia River fishery. At the same time both legislatures sought, less successfully, to deal with another group that was infringing on the salmon resource. These were trollers.

In the early 1900s, when marine gasoline engines became available, some gillnetters began trolling for salmon. Indians had trolled for salmon, and fishermen off Monterey, California, had discovered that chinook and coho salmon would bite at a baited hook or lure. The marine gasoline engine enabled fishermen to cross the Columbia River bar to fish for salmon during the closed season from August 25 to September 10. At this time Oregon and Washington had not extended their fisheries control to three miles from shore, nor had they enacted laws to control deliveries of fishers to buying stations. The demand for salmon was strong, and fishermen went trolling to catch fish.

Trolling was not highly regarded as a fishing technique. The arguments against it were that immature fish were harvested, fish spoiled in transport from the trolling grounds to the cannery, and salmon that were hooked and not landed died as a result of their wounds. C. H. Gilbert, a scientist from Stanford University, wrote the Columbia River Fishermen's League in 1921 on trolling for salmon: "It was an economic waste to take them before they had attained their full size."[39] The chance to exclude trollers, however, evaded legislators. After World War II this activity became more important and increased its impact on Columbia River fish runs.

*　*　*　*

All of the fishers, using a variety of gear, competed for salmon coming into the Columbia River. What were the number of units fishing, the quantity caught, and the ratio of their catch?

The first major study of the canned salmon industry was conducted for the years 1889-1892.[40] The purpose of the study was to assess the causes for decline in the salmon pack from 630,000 cases in 1883 to 310,000 cases in 1889. Additional studies were conducted in 1904, 1909, and 1915. Since 1923, the annual report, *Fisheries Industries of the United States,* has provided data on gear fished and catch. To provide a base for contrasting the effects of legislation restricting various types of fishers, the following three periods are compared: (1) 1889 to 1892; (2) 1904, 1909, and 1915; and (3) 1930 to 1934. The 1930-1934 period is comparable to the late 1920s. Tables 3, 4, and 5 show the number of units fished, catch per unit, and relative percentage of the catch for these three periods.

1889 to 1892. In this period the number of gillnets remained nearly constant, at an average of 1,240. The number of traps more than doubled— from 164 to 378. Haul seines and fishwheels averaged 40 and 45, respectively. Dipnets dropped from 110 to 75. This was a period of readjustment after the peaks of 1883 and 1884. Gillnetters took more than half the catch. The remainder was made by trapmen, fishwheelers, seiners, and dipnetters, in that order. There were no trollers.

---

[37] Jens Nielsen to Herbert Hoover, U.S. Food Administrator (Portland, Oregon Historical Society), MSS 1699, Box 6.

[38] J. G. Megler to Herbert Hoover, Secretary of Commerce, June 25, 1917 (Portland, Oregon Historical Society), MSS 1699, Box 6.

[39] Charles H. Gilbert to Columbia River Fishermen's League, October 6, 1921 (Portland, Oregon Historical Society), MSS 1699, Box 6.

[40] William A. Wilcox, "Fisheries of the Pacific Coast," *Report of the Commissioner of Fish and Fisheries for the Year Ending June 30, 1893* (Washington, D.C., 1895).

Table 3. Numbers of Columbia River Gear Fished

	Period		
Gear	1889-1892	1904, 1909, 1915	1930-1934
	Number		
Gillnet	1,240	2,660	1,330
Trap	240	350	400
Seine	40	70	80
Fishwheel	45	50	35
Dipnet	90		
Troll	0	500 (1915)	

SOURCE: Calculated from William A. Wilcox, "Fisheries of the Pacific Coast," *Report of the Commissioner of Fish and Fisheries for the Year Ending June 30, 1893* (Washington, D.C., 1895), pp. 157-161; William A. Wilcox, *The Commercial Fisheries of the Pacific Coast States in 1904* (Washington, D.C., 1907), Bureau of Fisheries Document No. 612, pp. 33-49; John N. Cobb, *The Salmon Fisheries of the Pacific Coast* (Washington, D.C., 1911), Bureau of Fisheries Document No. 751, pp. 84, 86, 91, 99-100; Lewis Radcliffe, *Fishing Industries of the United States* (Washington, D.C., 1919), Bureau of Fisheries Document No. 875, pp. 66-122.

Table 4. Average Poundage of Salmon and Steelhead Caught by Columbia River Gear

	Period		
Gear	1889-1892	1904, 1909, 1915	1930-1934
	pounds/unit		
Gillnet	12,300	7,300	10,200
Trap	25,300	20,700	12,400
Seine	60,100	75,100	47,100
Fishwheel	89,700	47,400	12,700

SOURCE: Same as Table 3.

Table 5. Percentage of Catch by Each Type of Columbia River Gear

	Period		
Gear	1889-1892	1904, 1909, 1915	1930-1934
	percent		
Gillnet	54	56	51
Trap	22	21	18
Seine	9	14	14
Fishwheel	14	7	2
Dipnet	2		2
Troll	0	5 (1915)	12
TOTAL HARVEST (million lbs.)	27.7	35.0	27.4

SOURCE: Same as Table 3.

1904, 1909, and 1915. During this period seiners surpassed the take of fishwheelers. The decline in fishwheel catch was caused by overfishing of blueback runs. Bluebacks made up 45 percent of the fishwheel catch in the 1889-1892 period, but declined to 21 percent during this period. Coupled with the decline in blueback runs was an increase in the chinook catch by seiners. From 1889 to 1892, seines averaged 1.7 million pounds of chinook per year. In 1904, 1909, and 1915, the average was 3.5 million pounds.

1930 to 1934. In this period gillnetters continued to take half the catch, with half the number of gillnets previously used. The number of traps increased and their average catch declined. Further, loss of habitat in the watershed caused salmon runs to decline after 1930. Fewer salmon were available, and the relative catch of trollers increased in the 1930-1934 period. Their catch was nearly equal to that of the seiners. The fishwheel catch had become nearly insignificant, partially because Oregon passed an initiative petition eliminating fishwheels on the Oregon side of the Columbia.

Tables 3, 4, and 5 show how fishers were taking one another's fish. Fishermen took either from those fishing with the same type of gear or from those with competing gear types. The number of gillnets doubled during the second period, resulting in a decrease of the average gillnet catch. The increase in troller catches from 1930 to 1934 caused declines in the catches of gillnetters, trapmen, and fishwheelers.

These facts were known to the fishermen. Gillnetters from Astoria knew that the trapmen in Baker Bay were competing with them for fish and fishing space. The trapmen and gillnetters were aware of the competition by the cannery-owned seines. The lower river fishermen were aware of the competition with the upriver fishwheelers and dipnetters. Each group of fishers was competing for a limited resource, and fishers within each group competed to take one another's fish.

Fishers also recognized the many mechanisms for taking one another's fish—intimidation, legislation, initiative petitions, and their own innovativeness. Also, most of the fishers were immigrants, and attempts were made to exclude them because they were aliens. After World War I laws were passed requiring those wanting to obtain a fishing license to be a citizen or to declare their intention to become one. The problem was described by Fred Barker, general manager of the Columbia River Packers Association, "These men are residents and have been for many years, but on account of their lack of education they will never be able to qualify, but what they lack in education they have always made up by hard work."[41] Unfortunately, hard work was not enough when resources were scarce. Numerous attempts were made to exclude aliens from fishing for salmon. Citizenship was made a condition for obtaining a license. This method of exclusion was not particularly successful since canneries purchased licenses for fishermen, fishermen lied about their status, and fishermen sought to obtain licenses where restrictions were less stringently enforced. Alien exclusion did not pit one fishing group against another, although gillnetters were most affected; instead, it pitted fishermen who were citizens against immigrants who had not become citizens.

[41] Fred Barker to W. S. Burnett, Hammond Lumber Company, January 24, 1924 (Portland, Oregon Historical Society), MSS 1699, Box 6.

Chapter 5/

Highliners

"HIGHLINERS" are people who catch the most fish. Every fisherman strives to be a highliner. Each day in cafes, bars, and coffee shops fishermen compared their receipts and identified those who caught the most fish. Some, such as "Highline Hansen," were consistently at the top. On the night of June 23, 1896, after the strike settlement, Frank Mercurio was high man with 7,000 pounds![1] Highliners for the season were also identified. Chris Christensen was high man in 1904 with 46,000 pounds. The *Pacific Fisherman* reported, "Every season the question of who will be the 'high boat' rests between the same dozen fishermen, . . . but they all take awful chances by fishing on the bar and often outside."[2] In 1913, Ben Johnson had the high boat, with 46,800 pounds. Eigrald Eide was his puller. Johnson netted $1,600 and Eide $875.[3]

Gillnetters were most numerous among the Columbia River commercial salmon fishers. From two gillnets and four gillnetters in 1866, their number increased rapidly.[4] The number of gillnets known or estimated to have been fished from 1874 to 1973 is shown in Figure 1. The number of gillnets increased to 1,650 in 1883 and then declined as the salmon pack declined. A second peak was reached in 1915 when about 2,800 gillnets were used. The number of gillnets and boats declined after World War I. The decline was caused by a manpower shortage during the war and by the postwar depression.

Prior to 1900 gillnets were fished by a captain who handled the net and the boat puller who rowed the boat. With increased use of gasoline engines, one man could handle a gillnet boat. By 1928 the total number of gillnet boats was one-half that of 1915 and the number of one-man boats exceeded the number of two-man boats. By the mid-1930s two-thirds were one-man boats. In 1973 only a few two-man boats were still operating; most boats were one-man.

The Columbia River gillnet boat prior to 1900 was sail powered. It was described by Captain Joshua Slocum as "a double-ender, carvel-built and fitted with a centerboard, her dimensions were length 25 feet, beam 6 feet, depth 2 feet 6 inches." The sail power was "a single 16-foot mast, to carry a spritsail."[5] Around 1900, gasoline engines replaced the sail power. The early marine gas engines were far from reliable, described as "the most 'ornary animale' that ever escaped from the menagerie." Salmon canner H. S. McGowan wrote, "The poor devil of a buyer not only had to bear all of the expense of finding out the faults of the critter, but

[1] *Daily Astorian,* June 23, 1896, p. 1.
[2] *Pacific Fisherman* 2 (October 1904), p. 15.
[3] *Pacific Fisherman* 11 (September 1913), p. 62.
[4] Columbia River Fishermen's Protective Union, Pamphlet (Astoria, 1890), p. 12.

[5] Victor Slocum, *Captain Joshua Slocum, The Life and Voyages of America's Best Known Sailor* (Astoria, Columbia River Maritime Museum), pp. 41-42.

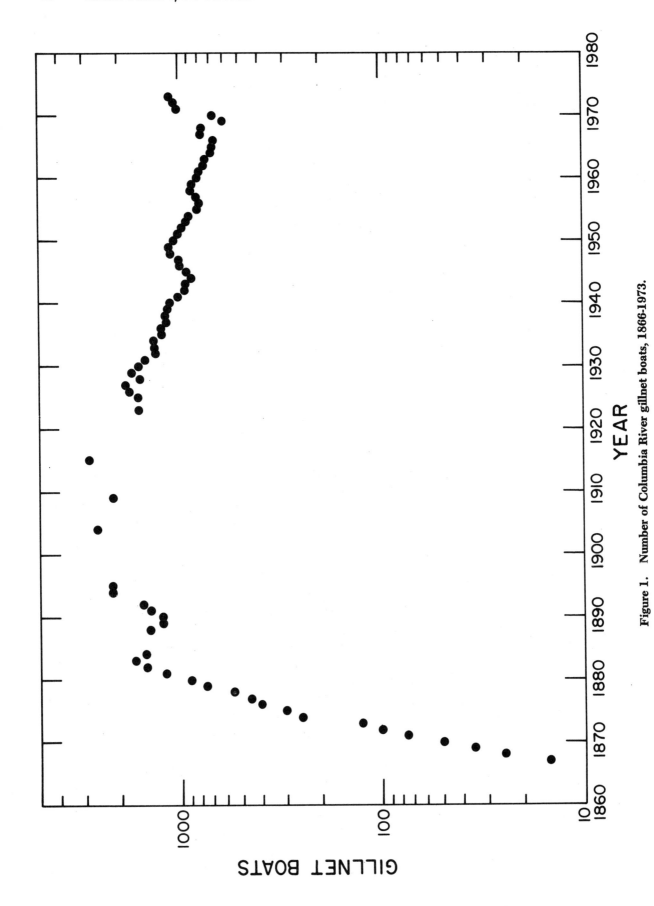

Figure 1.   Number of Columbia River gillnet boats, 1866-1973.

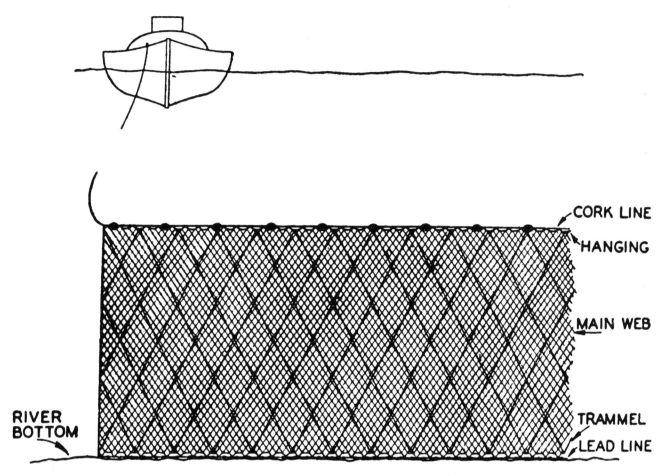

Method of fishing a diver net (Joseph A. Craig and Robert L. Hacker, "The History and Development of the Fisheries of the Columbia River," *Bulletin of the Bureau of Fisheries* 49, 1940, p. 167).

to fix up the damages, and pocket the incidental loss of time and opportunity."[6] The early models were improved. In 1912, the Columbia River Packers Association advanced money to buy gas engines to many of its fishermen. General Manager George H. George said, "We can't fish without the most improved methods in appliances."[7] By 1915, the sail power had been completely replaced by gasoline engines.

The early gillnets fished best at night when fish had greater difficulty seeing them. When the river was high and muddy, gillnets could fish during the day. The gillnets used by Hapgood, Hume and Company were floater nets, meaning their cork

[6] H. S. McGowan to John Fox, November 22, 1918 (Seattle, University of Washington), Cobb Papers, Box 1.

[7] George H. George to A. B. Hammond, May 30, 1912 (Portland, Oregon Historical Society), MSS 1699, Box 5.

line floated on the top of the water and the lead line stretched the net to a depth of 23 feet. The net was 750 feet long. Mesh size measured 8 to 8¼ inches when stretched. Many improvements were made in the construction of gillnets. Diver gillnets, whose lead line moved along the bottom of the river, were introduced about 1900. These nets were developed to catch the large chinook salmon, those over 25 pounds, which were usually worth 1 to 2 cents more per pound. The large salmon were mild-cured and sold mainly in northern European markets. The trammel net, a large mesh net placed behind the gillnet, was also used to catch large salmon. When large salmon hit the gillnet, they often were not gilled and escaped. The trammel net caused the gillnet to form a bag in which the large salmon was caught. When contacting the

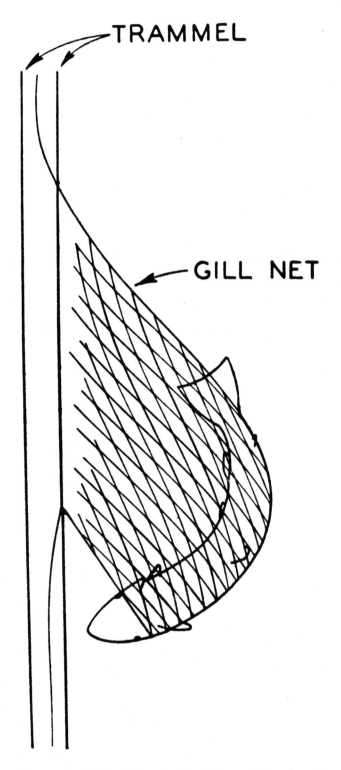

TRAMMEL

GILL NET

Manner in which a fish pulls the gillnet webbing through a trammel mesh, thus forming a bag (Joseph A. Craig and Robert L. Hacker, "The History and Development of the Fisheries of the Columbia River," *Bulletin of the Bureau of Fisheries* 49, 1940, p. 167).

gillnet, large salmon sometimes backed out before being gilled or enclosed in the bag created by the trammel. An apron net was added to the cork line to prevent the ungilled salmon from swimming over the diver net. Salmon fishers have continued to improve their gear. They have adopted stronger and less visible net materials and new methods for hanging nets to catch as many salmon as possible.

Gillnetters of the late nineteenth century were a hard-living group. Most migrated from the Sacramento River-San Francisco area for the April 1 to August 1 fishing season. Saturday night was their night off, and the January 1, 1882, *Oregonian* characterized these Saturday nights in Astoria as "a grand debauch for all the privations and hardships of the week." During the fishing season Astoria was characterized as "the most wicked place on earth for its population."[8] Some fishermen, "addicted to drinking bad whiskey," did not wait for Saturday night, but traded their fish at the whiskey scows on the river. The June 27, 1894, *Astorian Daily Budget* reported that the fishermen "spent most of their time and all of their money in these floating man-traps, where they barter their good fish for the vilest kind of rot-gut."[9]

In his memoirs, Captain Peter Johnson provides a sketch of one of the hard-living Columbia River gillnetters.[10] In 1883 Johnson hired on as a boat puller for "a man they called 'Laughing Pete.'" Laughing Pete was "considered the nerviest, as well as the best, fisherman on the lower Columbia River." He was never satisfied unless his net was out in front of the others. Johnson recounts that one afternoon "we were drifting toward the bar with a strong ebb tide, when I suggested that we pick up the net as I doubted that we could hold it in the breakers." But the net was briefly lost in the breakers. Soon it was retrieved, salmon and all. Johnson then "ran for the mast, hoisted the sail, and with a strong wind blowing from the sea" began to sail upriver. The boat was caught by a breaker and half-filled with water. Johnson

[8] *Oregonian*, January 1, 1882, p. 1.

[9] *Astorian Daily Budget*, June 27, 1894, p. 1.

[10] *Memoirs of Captain Peter Johnson*, facsimile copy of No. 185 (San Francisco Maritime Museum), pp. 17-19.

grabbed a lunch bucket, emptied its contents over the side, and started bailing out the water. When they reached the cannery and picked the salmon from their net, they "found that we had caught eighty-five, which brought seventy-five cents apiece." Since it was eleven at night, Johnson was ready, after his narrow escape, for a good sleep, but Laughing Pete wanted to celebrate on the town. He told Johnson to meet him at two o'clock the next afternoon. "When Pete got there, one look assured me," said Johnson, "that he was loaded for fair, but he came aboard telling me to get the line and pull out to the river." Johnson said he was "dubious as to the wisdom of going with a drunken man, but as he was one of the best-natured men I'd ever met, and since he had no liquor with him, I thought he would soon sober up." In the 18-mile distance from Astoria to the bar Pete did sober up. They fished in conditions the same as the day before, but "this time the net stopped before it got into the breakers." Their haul was 34 salmon. They then went to Fort Stevens to cook salmon-head chowder for supper. After spending the night there, they fished the next morning on the ebb tide and caught 17 more salmon. Johnson says, "I began to figure my income. I would make so much money that I would not know what to do with it. I received thirty-five cents per salmon and 'Laughing Pete' forty cents."

The fish were sold either directly to canners or to cash buyers. If a gillnetter sold directly to cash buyers, he was paid cash for the quantity of fish sold. The cash buyers did not extend credit or offer other incentives to obtain the gillnetter's catch. Gillnetters selling to canneries received a lower price than that paid by the cash buyers. The benefits in selling to the canneries were credit on the purchase of gear and equipment, cash advances, and sometimes a year-end bonus for fishing for the same cannery all season. Because of the credit and cash advanced, canneries kept detailed records on the accounts of fishermen. Many of these accounts have been preserved, and they provide a basis for analyzing how well a gillnetter could do.

✻　✻　✻　✻

The income of fishers depended on the price set for fish. Each spring, prior to the salmon season, canners and fishermen made their respective price offers. The union voted on the price it would ask. Canners offered the price at which they thought they could make a profit given a pessimistic outlook for the season. This early in the season, canners were uncertain what price their pack would bring. The market price fluctuated, depending on the amount unsold from the previous season, the pack in other areas, the run size, and the strength of the market. With these unknowns, canners tried to keep the price as low as possible.

Once a price was agreed to, fishermen sold their fish at that price. When the run peaked and canners had little trouble obtaining fish, the price was usually cut. Salmon prices distinguished between large and small salmon. Those weighing more than 25 pounds generally received 1 to 2 cents more per pound. Large salmon of the best quality were mild-cured. Smaller salmon were canned. Here, too, when supplies were abundant the price differential was not held. For example, a 1911 letter from the Columbia River Packers Association to their Desdemona fish-buying station stated, "You will notice that the price of fish on the 16th instant Wednesday morning, becomes 6 cents per pound both large and small salmon." The station man was instructed, "The fish will be weighed together as cannery salmon so far as the fishermen are concerned, but we want you to pick out the largest and the best chinooks and put them in boxes and send them to the Cold Storage Plant."[11]

The spring price was always the highest. If the spring run was a very good one, the canneries closed and did not operate during the fall. When the spring runs were poor, fall chinook salmon were packed, usually as a lower grade of salmon. Fall fish prices were about one-third of the spring season price.

The price received by gillnetters is constructed from two sources: (1) the price negotiated for the opening of the spring season and (2) the average price received for spring chinook salmon (Appendix B). Figure 2 shows a general increase in the corrected price paid to fishermen. The points

[11] Columbia River Packers Association memo to Desdemona Station, August 14, 1911 (Portland, Oregon Historical Society), MSS 1699, Box 8.

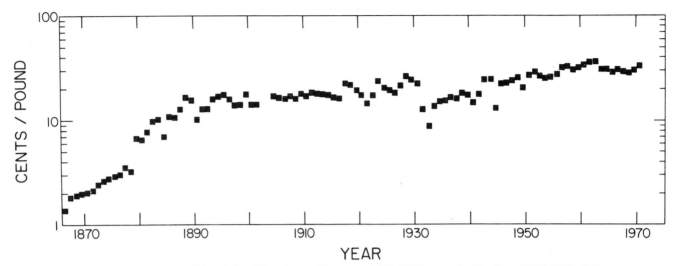

Figure 2. **Price received by Columbia River gillnetters, 1866-1971, standardized to 1957-1959 dollars.**

in the figure have been standardized to 1957-1959 prices. Dips caused by depressions occurred in 1921 and 1932. Peaks are associated with wars, e.g., 1917-1918 and 1942-1944. The prices received by the fishermen increased when there was a strong union, e.g., 1886 to 1889, 1928 to 1929, and 1933. The fish price does not correlate with the size of the pack or the prices received by the canners for their pack, suggesting that canners controlled fish prices.

One factor which counterbalanced the price control power of canners was the cash buyers. Cash buyers bought salmon in competition with the canneries. The price they offered was higher because they did not provide the services offered by the canneries. During times of strong demand for salmon, competition between the cash buyer and the cannery could drive up the prices paid fishers, as it did in 1923 and 1924.

How well could a gillnetter do fishing on the Columbia River? In looking at the well-being of gillnetters, a distinction must be made between how fishers perceive their well-being and how their well-being is measured against some economic criterion of performance. An economic measure of a fisher's well-being would take into account the relationship between costs and returns. The fisherman's definition of costs and returns, however, often differs from that of the economist. One fisherman summed it up by saying, "The true fisherman does not figure money. He figures catch and the money takes care of itself."

A typical economic analysis of fishermen's incomes includes variable, fixed, and opportunity costs.[12] Variable costs are for such things as fuel, bait, maintenance, and crew shares, the day-to-day expenses of catching fish. Fixed costs include licenses, interest, taxes, insurance, and depreciation on equipment. These are costs which the fisher will have whether he fishes or not. Opportunity costs include the operator's labor, management, and return to investment. An economic evaluation of a 28-foot Astoria gillnet boat for 1973 is shown in Table 6.[13] The table shows that the gillnetter, after paying fixed and variable costs, had only $2,327 to cover his labor, management, and return to investment.

Many fishers do not think of fishing in this economic sense. An old gillnetter comparing his 1972 earnings with those of 1917 said, "Then the standard of living was not as high, and there was nothing to spend your money on, except possibly the taverns." In fact, the more important thing for a gillnetter was to be a "highliner."

[12] Frederick J. Smith, *Understanding and Using Marine Economics Data Sheets* (1973), Marine Advisory Program, Oregon State University, SG 24.

[13] Frederick J. Smith, "28-Foot Astoria Salmon Gillnetter," *Marine Economics Data Sheet No. 3* (1973), Marine Advisory Program, Oregon State University, 1973.

Table 6. Economic Evaluation of 28-Foot Astoria
Salmon Gillnet Boat, 1973

Item	Value ($)
Variable costs	$6,441
Fixed costs	1,407
Opportunity costs	
Operator's labor (30% of gross)	3,053
Operator's management (10% of gross)	1,018
Interest on investment (at 9%)	878
Gross returns	10,175
Market value of boat and nets	9,755
Return to labor, management, and investment (gross less variable and fixed costs)	2,327
Return to investment (gross less fixed and variable costs, operator's labor and management)	−1,744

SOURCE: Frederick J. Smith, *Marine Economics Data Sheet No. 3* (1973), Oregon State University, Marine Advisory Program.

Usually fixed costs such as depreciation and opportunity costs such as returns to management and investment were not figured by fishermen. Most fishers were satisfied if enough money was left to satisfy their needs after paying their expenses. The definition of expenses and needs was an individual thing and varied from fisher to fisher. For many the compensations of fishing were other than monetary. For a violent man, fishing was a way of venting his violence. Fishing was a way for the individual to work out the conflict of man versus nature. It was a way of getting into one's self and working out personal problems. Fishing was a test of yourself and your capabilities. One salmon fisherman said, "Fishing is the only complete experience. When I come home I am totally satisfied, except I get really horny. Fishing uses everything I have—my mind, my body, and my spirit."

These factors are intangibles and are difficult to convert to a dollar value. Several studies have been conducted on the dollar success of gillnetters. In fact, the first analysis was made in 1890 by the gillnetters themselves to show there were too many fishermen, especially trapmen, seiners, and fishwheelers.[14] The report of the Columbia River Fishermen's Protective Union showed that gillnetter's wages had declined from an average daily wage of

[14] Columbia River Fishermen's Protective Union, 1890 (see note 4).

$5 in 1866 to around $2 per day. The calculation was made by dividing the number of fish caught by the number of boats. This was multiplied by the price paid per fish. One-third was subtracted from the gross for rent of net and boat.

For example, in 1883, one of the big years, 1,650 boats caught 1,568,000 salmon, or 950 per boat. The price that year was 85 cents per salmon, which provided the average boat with a gross income of $808. One-third of the gross was paid the cannery for expenses. This left $539 to be divided between the captain and his boat puller. The net income was $268.50 per man. The season was 4 months long, providing a monthly wage of $67.

After 1888 the canners refused the one-third rent formula and sold nets to the fishermen for $200 to $400. A net could be used for two to three seasons. Each year one-third of the net was re-tied with new twine. Boat rental was $50 per season. This pricing system operated against the casual, part-time fishermen and favored those who delivered a lot of fish.

John Mattson, one of the best known highliners, calculated average returns to gillnetters for 1895.[15] Mattson made $1,200 that year, but he was concerned with the level of fishermen's indebtedness to the canneries. He calculated that the average landings in 1895 were 13,400 pounds per boat. With salmon selling for 5 cents per pound, the average gross income was $670 per boat. Costs were estimated at $286, leaving a net income of $394 or an average wage for captain and puller of $50 per month for the spring season. Mattson thought this was a "poor wage because after deductions for board the fishermen would not have enough to pay for food and clothing." Added to this was the average indebtedness to the canneries calculated by Mattson at $151 per fisherman.

The next wage study was made in 1917 to provide information for implementing wage and price controls necessitated by World War I.[16] This study listed the average gillnetter's costs at $657 (Table 7). Depreciation and interest were new items in

[15] *Daily Astorian*, June 2, 1896, p. 4.
[16] Study located among 1918 letters of Fred Barker (Portland, Oregon Historical Society), MSS 1699, Box 6.

Table 7. Average Costs of Columbia River Gillnetter, 1917

Item	Expense ($)
Linen twine	$231.00
Cotton twine and line	32.00
Lead line and cork line	35.00
Boat repairs	15.00
Bluestone and tan	20.00
Annual repairs, 26 days at $4/day	104.00
Gas and oil	50.00
Licenses	10.00
Depreciation on boat	75.00
Interest on investment (9% on $950)	85.00
TOTAL	$657.00

SOURCE: Columbia River Packers Association, Oregon Historical Society, MSS 1699, Box 6.

the calculation, items which most fishermen and many canners at this time did not figure. In 1917, the boat captain owned the net and the boat. Expenses were charged against the captain's share. The typical share was 70 to 75 percent of the gross for the captain and 25 to 30 percent for the puller. The average gross income per boat was $1,527. This gave the boat captain an income of $124 per month after expenses were deducted, and the average boat puller received $93.50.

A 1925-1929 study estimated spring season expenses for one-man boats at $575.[17] This was $355 for gear, $125 for gas and oil, and $75 for depreciation. These data were for men fishing for the Union Fishermen's Cooperative Packing Company. The average gross income was $1,275. This provided the fisherman with an average monthly spring season income of $175.

Two studies estimated gillnetter income in 1969 and 1971.[18] A 1969 study by the Washington Department of Fisheries estimated average income

[17] Elizabeth M. Wyland, "A Study in Unionism with Special Reference to the Columbia River Fishermen's Protective Union," Master's thesis, University of Oregon, Eugene, 1930, p. 62.
[18] Robert C. Lewis, *Preliminary Economic Analysis of Management Alternatives for Limiting Harvest Effort by Oregon Commercial Fisheries* (Portland, Fish Commission of Oregon, 1973), mimeo; and Stephen B. Mathews and Henry O. Wendler, *Relative Efficiency and Economic Yield of the Columbia River Drift Gill Net and Indian Set Net Fisheries,* (1970) Washington Department of Fisheries, Technical Report No. 3.

Table 8. Average Costs of Columbia River Gillnetter, 1969[a]

Item	Average ($)	Range ($)
Initial investment		
Vessel	$4,503	$700–16,500
Drift right	1,256	25– 3,500
Average	5,309	
Opportunity costs		
0.045 × 5,309	239	
Variable costs		
Parts	832	150– 2,500
Fuel	294	58– 2,500
Other[b] (dues, transportation, net storage, meals)	138	0– 4,000
Fixed costs		
Nets	1,133	
Depreciation	139	
Insurance	69	0– 300
Moorage	59	0– 400
License	57	35– 125
TOTAL variable and fixed costs	$2,721	

SOURCE: Stephen B. Mathews and Henry O. Wendler, *Relative Efficiency and Economic Yield of the Columbia River Drift Gill Net and Indian Set Net Fisheries* (1970), Washington Department of Fisheries, Technical Report No. 3, p. 10.

[a] Based on 30 returned questionnaires.
[b] $4,000, boat puller expense. This "other" category is a mixture of variable and fixed costs. Mathews and Wendler used the term "annual costs" in their table.

from total catch times the price received. The total gross income was divided by the number of gillnetters. The estimate of average gross income was $3,700. Fixed and variable costs were determined from a survey of 30 gillnetters (Table 8). The average net income was $980. In 1971 the Fish Commission of Oregon attempted to obtain income data for gillnetters. Their estimate was based on the landings of 459 Oregon licensed gillnetters. Gross income averaged $2,900. No estimate was made of the cost of fishing. Using the two-thirds of gross income to cost ratio found in the Washington study, net income would be $960. This is comparable to the figure obtained by the Washington Department of Fisheries. The Oregon highliners in 1971 grossed more than $18,000.

These figures on gillnetters' incomes for 1866, 1883, 1895, 1917, 1925-1929, and 1969-1971 are standardized to 1957-1959 dollars, and the average

Mast and sail provide gillnetters shelter while waiting for evening tide (Weister photo, Oregon Historical Society).

net income was never substantial (Table 9). The very first year and the boom during World War I were the best income years. These were also times when mostly two-man boats were operated. To get

Table 9. Income per Gillnet, Columbia River Salmon Fishery

Year	Average gross income/ gillnet ($)	Average fixed & variable costs ($)	Average net income/ gillnet ($)	Net income (1957-1959 dollars)[a] ($)
1866	$ 900	[b]	$ 900	$1,760
1883	810	270	540	1,640
1895	670	290	380	1,410
1917	1,660	111	1,000	2,240
1925-1929	1,270	570	700	1,160
1969-1971	3,300	2,330	970	720

[a] Calculated using consumer price index, all commodities in the U.S. Department of Labor, Bureau of Labor Statistics, *Handbook of Labor Statistics, 1972,* Bulletin No. 1790, p. 290.

[b] Costs of fishing not reported. Calculation of net income based on assumption that boat and net were owned by the cannery. This was the most common pattern during the early years of the fishery.

the average net income per fisherman, the 1866, 1883, 1895, and 1917 net incomes per gillnet have to be divided in half. Thus, shortly after the establishment of the salmon industry gillnetters faced the problem of too many fishermen competing for fish. The four gillnetters in 1866 increased to 3,300 in 1883. Their average monthly wage decreased from more than $100 to under $70. The average net income levels (Table 9) do not point to gill-netting being a full-time occupation for the majority of fishermen.

The part-time nature of gillnetting was noted in the 1880s. G. B. Goode observed that less than one-tenth of the fishermen came from the towns where they were employed. Most came from San Francisco. Some owned farms. Finns migrated from the mines in Montana for the fishing season.[19] Writing in 1903 about the fishermen staying in Astoria, Alfred Cleveland observed: "During the win-

[19] Larry Skoog, "The Great Sand Island War," February 14, 1973 (Tape of talk to Clatsop County Historical Society, Astoria Public Library).

Sail-powered gillnet boat, near Astoria (Oregon Historical Society).

ter months most of the fishermen are employed carpentering, street building, as workers in the mills and factories or engaged in knitting nets and preparing gear for the next season."[20] Hunting seals and sea lions, who preyed on the salmon, was another activity. Logging and longshoring were two of the most important off-season occupations. In fact, fishing could be mixed with any occupation allowing time off to fish the peaks of the salmon runs. Teachers, firemen, policemen, truckdrivers, and many others fished part-time.

The part-time nature of the fishery was caused by the runs of salmon entering the river. Each run had a peak. Prior to 1900 the major peak occurred around June 20, and then the peak shifted to late July and early August. With greater pressure to fish the fall runs, the early September run was fished. Fall fishing also extended the season. Prior to 1900 the season was 100 to 120 days, with most of the fishing completed by early August. More runs were fished after 1900 and the season increased in length. During the 1930s the season lasted more than 250 days. Management efforts to maintain declining run sizes reduced the season to 225 days in the 1940s, to 150 days in the 1950s, and to 85 days in the 1960s.[21] The shortening of the seasons continued in the 1970s, forcing those who wanted to fish full time to go to other areas. Alaska was the most common choice. Fishing for other species was another alternative.

*   *   *   *

These discussions of what was average or typical do not indicate the important character of the highliner—he caught more than the average

[20] Alfred A. Cleveland, "Social and Economic History of Astoria," *Oregon Historical Quarterly* 4 (June 1903), pp. 148-149.

[21] Fish Commission of Oregon and Washington Department of Fisheries, *Status Report, Columbia River Fish Runs and Commercial Fisheries, 1938-70, 1974 Addendum* (Portland, 1975), p. 18.

amount of fish. Therefore, in addition to discussing what is average, the distribution of the catch among fishermen is important. To look at the distribution of the catch, variations from the average must be evaluated. Data for 1899, 1916-1925, and 1971 indicate the distribution of income among gillnetters.

Table 10 was constructed from the incomes of Columbia River Packers Association gillnetters for 1899 and 1916-1925.[22] These data include both captains and pullers. Data for 1971 came from licensed Oregon gillnetters fishing the Columbia River.[23]

Table 10. Average Income of Columbia River Gillnetters

Year	Average income per individual (1957-1959 dollars)	Skewing[a]	Peaking[b]
1899	$390 (1,350)	0.62	0.70
1916-1925	970 (1,710)	0.90	0.78
1971	2,900 (2,060)	1.78	3.87

SOURCE: Columbia River Packers Association, Oregon Historical Society, MSS 1699, Box 139.

[a] Higher positive values for skewing indicate that few gillnetters' incomes are well above average; most of their incomes fall below average.

[b] Higher values for peaking indicate concentration of incomes. For 1971, these data indicate that the majority of gillnetters' incomes concentrated below the average, while in 1899, incomes were more evenly distributed about the average.

The distribution of gillnetter incomes is compared with that of a normal distribution in Figure 3. If gillnetter incomes were distributed normally, the number of incomes above average would equal the number of incomes below average. Incomes would concentrate around the mean. If gillnetter incomes were normally distributed, there should be no skewing or peaking. Values for skewing and peaking should be near zero.

[22] Fishermen's Trial Balances, 1899 Ledger Book, and 30 percent sample from Fishermen's Trial Balances 1916-1925 (Portland, Oregon Historical Society), MSS 1699, Boxes 38 and 39.

[23] Joe B. Stevens, personal communication.

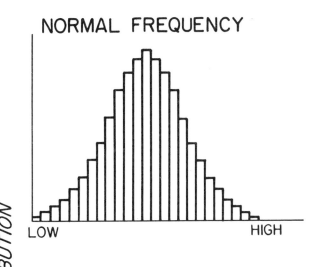

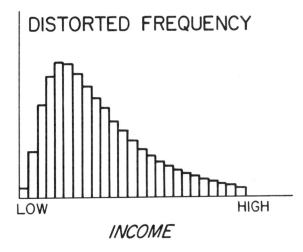

Figure 3. Normal and distorted income distributions.

Skewing and peaking were greatest in 1971 (Table 10). This indicates that most gillnetters had incomes below average in 1971 and only a few did very well. The income distribution in this situation takes on the distorted shape shown in Figure 3. The greater distortion indicates a situation in which too many fishermen were competing with one another for salmon. Most did poorly relative to the average.

This problem can be elaborated by looking more closely at the 1916-1925 period. World War I increased the demand for canned salmon, a depression occurred in 1921, and then conditions improved. Prior to the war, gillnetters were doing poorly (Table 11). The 1916 distribution shows distortion of gillnetter incomes toward many doing poorly relative to the average and only a few doing very well. The skew and peaking values were greater than 1.0. Demand for canned salmon stimulated by the war led to a more even distribution (skewing and peaking values closer to 0). The

Table 11.   Income of Columbia River Packers Association Gillnetters, 1916-1925

Year	Average income per individual	Skew[a]	Peaking[b]
1916	$ 580	1.14	1.14
1917	820	1.22	1.41
1918	1,130	0.89	0.59
1919	1,010	0.49	−0.27
1920	1,340	0.60	−0.28
1921	700	1.64	5.42
1922	800	0.93	0.44
1923	1,280	0.70	−0.14
1924	890	0.71	−0.15
1925	1,130	0.66	−0.36

Source: Columbia River Packers Association, Oregon Historical Society, MSS 1699, Box 39.

[a] Higher positive values for skewing indicate that few gillnetters' incomes are well above average; most of their incomes fall below average.

[b] Higher values for peaking indicate concentration of income.

Alaska salmon pack was poor in 1920, delaying the effects of the postwar depression on the Columbia River. In 1921, the postwar depression caused the

fishermen's income distribution to more closely resemble that of prewar times. Manpower requirements during World War I kept the number of fishermen from increasing until 1920, when many newcomers entered the industry. The newcomers were less successful than experienced fishermen, and the 1921 depression caused many of them to drop out of the fishery. More than 130 association gillnetters who fished in 1921 did not fish in 1922. The average 1921 catch for the dropouts was only 70 percent of the catch for the experienced fisherman. The depression resulted in excluding unsuccessful fishermen. After the 1921 depression, demand and fish prices improved, and the gillnetter's income distribution became more similar to distribution after World War I when salmon demand was strong.

The 1916-1925 period provides a short-term example of how, when the market for salmon is limited and more fishers are seeking to profit from the fishery than it can sustain, the majority of fishermen have incomes below the average and only a few do well. Since the 1930s, decline has been the trend in the canned salmon industry. The question, then, becomes: What are some of the correlates with this trend? One appears to be that more fishermen's incomes are concentrated below the average. The implications of this are that more benefits are being sought from the fishery than it can provide.

Chapter 6/

Cannery Manager

FISHERS WERE FIRST in the chain that provided fish for the consumer. The cannery manager, as intermediary in the chain, looked both ways. On one hand, cannery managers were concerned with the well-being of their fishermen and, on the other hand, with running their business at a profit. The cannery owners sought to profit from hauling in the nets and processing the salmon.

Free enterprise was one of the key objectives of the cannery manager. By incorporating innovations to increase productivity, an effectively operating free enterprise system should improve the wages of workers, reduce prices to consumers, and maintain profitability for owners. During its first 20 years the Columbia River salmon fishery worked this way. The demands for higher wages for fishers and lower costs for consumers were met during the early development of the fishery by innovations in processing, in fish catching, and in cannery management.

During the 1880s, canners faced a cost-price squeeze. Profits for many were insufficient and a number dropped out. The number of Columbia River canneries dropped from a high of 40 in 1883 to 24 in 1896. Those canners with the best fishing locations, canning facilities, and the most innovative management stayed in business.

By the 1890s, cannery managers were facing the dual problems of market saturation and a well-organized, effective union of fishermen. The Co-

lumbia River Fishermen's Protective Union organized most gillnetters on the river. The union was successful in obtaining higher fish prices for its members, and thereby mitigating the economic pressure on fishermen whose average catches were decreasing.

* * * *

Despite much talking, the canners remained too individualistic to organize a more united front for dealing with the union's demands. The union's strike of 1896 was an important stimulus for canners to think about consolidating cannery operations. Fishermen in 1896 set their price at 5 cents per pound. Canners argued they could not afford more than 4 cents. In March 1896, cannerymen met in Portland but failed to unite after "a great deal of elocution."[1] By forming a packers' association they had hoped to gain better control of the price paid fishermen and to increase the price paid for their product. The packers' failure to agree helped fishers maintain their power to ask for higher fish prices.

The fishermen, under the leadership of the Columbia River Fishermen's Protective Union, held out for their price. The union secretary, Sofus Jensen, explained that the union price demand was because of decreased fish runs. To maintain their incomes, fishermen needed to receive more for fewer fish caught. To the union, the reduced fish

[1] *Morning Astorian*, March 24, 1896, p. 1.

runs were caused by the competing seines and fishwheels owned by the canneries. Also at stake, then, was the union's desire to obtain a larger share of the catch for its fishermen. Jensen said, "not until it is arranged to do away with small mesh gear, wheels, and traps can there be expected any protection to Columbia river fish."[2]

The strike began in April. In a "great meeting held yesterday at Fishermen's Hall by all classes of fishermen, 2,000 fishermen decided 'it's five cents or nothing'" (*Daily Morning Astorian*, April 9, 1896). The strike dragged on into June, and there were threats and acts of violence. The union established three committees, "one to look after trapmen, one to watch the seines, and the other to see that the gillnet fishermen lived up to the agreement" not to fish. The National Guards of Oregon and Washington were called out to preserve order. The Washington National Guard ran out of money and had to return home, and then the Oregon Guard also withdrew.[3]

On June 5 fishermen asked the cannerymen to prove they could not make money at 5 cents per pound. The fishermen suggested the formation of a blue ribbon committee to study the question. Canneryman B. A. Seaborg spoke to the fishermen in Finnish and English on June 7 to explain his position as a canner. The 900 fishermen attending the meeting laughed at Seaborg's explanation. The Astoria Chamber of Commerce entered the dispute as an arbitrator on June 13. Finally, on June 23, fishing was resumed with the fish price at 4½ cents per pound. Each side felt that it had made its point.

The 1896 strike demonstrated to the canners the value of working together. Finally in 1899, seven Columbia River canning companies joined in a new corporation consolidating 10 canneries. They included Samuel Elmore, George H. George, William H. Barker, M. J. Kinney, J. O. Hanthorn, B. A. Seaborg, and J. W. Cook. They used only three of the canneries. William Barker was general manager, George H. George was secretary, and Samuel Elmore was vice president.

The idea for consolidating canneries was not a new one. Most canners had either witnessed or participated in the formation of the Alaska Packers Association, which was incorporated in 1893. The canneries operating in Alaska in 1891 packed far in excess of the market for their product. Therefore, in 1892, 31 of 37 canners formed a loose association, the Alaska Packing Association, to reduce the quantity packed and to sell the held-over pack. Samuel Elmore, then mayor of Astoria and an APA director, told the *San Francisco Examiner*, "It is our intention to pack about 400,000 cases in 1892."[4] The plan was to run only about nine canneries and divide the profits among the participants. The experiment worked successfully, and the next year the Alaska Packers Association was incorporated. It was the largest packing company on the Pacific Coast at that time and continued to be so.

The Columbia River Packers Association was a little different than the Alaska Packers Association. On the Columbia River enough capital was secured to buy out the interests of many of the cannery owners. Canners who joined received cash and/or stock in the new company for their assets.

* * * *

When the Columbia River Packers Association began, Samuel Elmore was vice president and manager of the company. Elmore was killed in an automobile accident in 1910 and George H. George took over management. George died in October 1913 and Fred Barker became general manager. Much of the correspondence and corporate records for the George - Barker period have been preserved. These records provide background on the decisions required for operating the Columbia River Packers Association from 1910 to 1924 when the association's president, A. B. Hammond, sold his controlling interest to William F. Thompson.

Hammond was the second largest stockholder, with 19 percent of the 17,250 shares. Only Mrs. Elmore owned more, 23 percent.[5] Hammond was a lumber entrepreneur whose company was headquartered in San Francisco. As general managers

[2] *Daily Astorian*, May 9, 1896.

[3] Larry Skoog, "The Great Sand Island War," February 14, 1973 (Tape of talk to Clatsop County Historical Society, Astoria Public Library).

[4] *San Francisco Examiner*, January 8, 1892.

[5] Columbia River Packers Association Stockholders, May 22, 1914 (Portland, Oregon Historical Society), MSS 1699, Box 23.

of the association, George H. George and Fred Barker reported association activities to Hammond, sometimes as often as weekly. Hammond's interests were on money matters and not the technical decisions on how to run a cannery.

Hammond directed the loaning and borrowing of money, preparation of balance sheets, timing of financial transactions, and property transfers. Each season prior to World War I, the association borrowed from $250,000 to $450,000 to put up the pack. Hammond watched the condition of the money market and secured these loans at the lowest possible rates. For example, Hammond wrote Barker in October 1915, "I look for hard times and a tight money market for sometime to come. I hope you will do everything you can to turn your product into money and to reduce your expenses to the utmost."[6]

The form of financial statements was also Hammond's particular concern. He told Barker in 1917, "We have obtained a very high credit through these banking statements, and it is largely due to the manner in which these statements are gotten out."[7] Hammond made changes to improve the statements, writing in 1921 that the category of "Bonds and Certificates" should be changed to "U.S. Treasury Certificates." He said, "Everybody knows that United States Treasury Certificates are equal to cash and Government bonds are a pretty good property and can be readily turned into cash and used as collateral, and besides it shows that you are the manager of a patriotic company that helped finance the government in its hour of need."[8]

The salary for the general manager of the Columbia River Packers Association was about $6,000 prior to World War I. George reported earnings of $4,583.33 for nine months of 1913, the first year incomes had to be reported for income tax purposes. Barker's salary was $6,000 for 1916. Hammond then raised his salary by $4,000, $3,000 of which was paid in stock.[9] Hammond wrote Barker in

1924, telling him of the sale of the association to William F. Thompson. He said that the company was worth considerably more than the amount Thompson and his associates paid, but "the fact that they have been able to induce you and your assistants to remain in the service of the company and pool your stock with theirs is a still greater asset."[10]

*   *   *   *

The management styles of George H. George and Fred Barker were quite different. George was usually optimistic, while Barker was more of a pessimist. The different personalities were reflected in the way business was conducted. For instance, when Barker took over as general manager in October 1913, he carried inventories at well below the selling price. George had carried inventories at the market price. Barker reduced the level of borrowing. To explain why no borrowings were required, he wrote, "Under ordinary conditions, we have been able in the past to finance ourselves without borrowing money through being able to ship out our Columbia River salmon as fast as our fishermen caught and delivered the fish to us."[11]

Barker, by his correspondence and management decisions, appeared to be a responsible businessman who recognized the role of business in the community. W. O. Barnes wrote in 1917 about the impact of new corporate taxes, "I assume it will hit the CRPA pretty hard, unless a goodly portion of said earnings are invested in Liberty Bonds."[12] Barker replied to Barnes, "We have understood all along that the only tax we would escape by the purchase of these Liberty Bonds would be on the undistributed surplus six months after the end of each calendar or fiscal year; in other words we would not escape any initial tax on our

[6] A. B. Hammond to Fred Barker, October 13, 1914 (Portland, Oregon Historical Society), MSS 1699, Box 22.

[7] A. B. Hammond to Fred Barker, March 18, 1917 (Portland, Oregon Historical Society), MSS 1699, Box 6.

[8] A. B. Hammond to Fred Barker, May 8, 1920 (Portland, Oregon Historical Society), MSS 1699, Box 6.

[9] Columbia River Packers Association, Income Tax Form 1031, December 31, 1916, and A. B. Hammond to Fred Barker, November 21, 1916 (Portland, Oregon Historical Society), MSS 1699, Boxes 43 and 6.

[10] A. B. Hammond to Fred Barker, October 18, 1924 (Portland, Oregon Historical Society), MSS 1699, Box 6.

[11] Fred Barker to A. B. Hammond, February 5, 1923 (Portland, Oregon Historical Society), MSS 1699, Box 6.

[12] W. O. Barnes to Fred Barker, October 17, 1917 (Portland, Oregon Historical Society), MSS 1699, Box 6.

FRED BARKER

General manager of Columbia River Packers Association, 1913-1928 (*Pacific Fisherman*, November 1912).

earnings. We figure that the Government has to have the money for the proper prosecution of the war, and they must raise it one way or the other."[13]

None of Barker's management decisions, however, can be characterized as altruistic. He recognized that Hammond and the association stockholders were interested in making a profit. His behavior in relations with other canners, with fishermen, with brokers, and with regulatory agencies was to maintain a profit-making business climate.

In addition to correspondence with Hammond, Barker had considerable contact with members of Hammond's organization and association stockholders. Barker's brother, William H. Barker, was president and general manager of the British Columbia Packers Association during Fred's tenure as Columbia River Packers Association general manager. William was also a major stockholder in the association. Fred and Will corresponded often, especially on market conditions. George B. McLeod headed Hammond's Oregon lumber operations. McLeod's office was in Portland, and Barker relied on him for his contacts with Portland businessmen and legislators.

When Barker became general manager in October 1913, he stepped into a situation in which

the association had butted into the territory of the Alaska Packers Association and the Northwestern Fisheries Company at Chignik in Alaska. George H. George wrote Hammond after the first year of operation in 1910, "We went up against a pretty hard proposition when we butted into Chignik," but he said, "I think we have demonstrated this year that we are able to take care of ourselves." Hammond replied, "You and Captain Osmund must see that your organization is placed on a war footing, and that Mr. Fortmann and his representatives find good fighting all along the line."[14] Such actions were costly. Each year the association lost money at Chignik because "war footing" meant increased costs of working there. Losses in 1913 were $60,000. This was because Alaska canneries required larger crews to compete for fish, and the crews had to leave earlier in the season to secure the fishing sites.

Barker quickly noticed this problem when he became general manager in October 1913, writing Hammond that the losses at Chignik were because "we have to take up so many men and so much gear in excess of what is actually required."[15] To get a jump on their competitors in trap site selection, crews left in December 1913 to prepare for the 1914 summer season. The three organizations reached agreement in January 1914, each of them receiving one-third of the fish caught. The settlement reduced the association's labor requirement from 100 fishermen to just over 30. This enabled profitable operations at Chignik for all the companies concerned. Knowing that these profits would continue only as long as there was cooperation, Barker wrote McCue of Northwestern Fisheries Company, "Your Captain Tagelder of the ship *St. Paul* is given too much to talk as to the fine opportunity for someone to come in and establish a small cannery at Chignik. While we do not like to mix in other people's employees," Barker wrote, "we believe it would be a good thing to shut the wind off Captain Tagelder, as we do not want to

[13] Fred Barker to W. O. Barnes, October 24, 1917 (Portland, Oregon Historical Society), MSS 1699, Box 6.

[14] George H. George to A. B. Hammond, September 28, 1911, and Hammond to George, January 16, 1912 (Portland, Oregon Historical Society), MSS 1699, Box 5.

[15] Fred Barker to A. B. Hammond, October 31, 1913 (Portland, Oregon Historical Society), MSS 1699, Box 22.

have increased costs at Chignik, if it is possible to avoid it."[16]

To pack a case of top grade chinook salmon in 1917, 55 percent of the cost was in acquisition of the fish (Table 12). The fishers, then, were one of the cannery manager's principal concerns. Since gillnetters landed most of the fish, they received most of the cannery manager's attention. To get the fish, Barker stated, "You have either got to do one of two things—make advances, or pay a cash price and a higher price than the other packers." The association policy was to make advances. Cash advances were used to live on during the off-season and for purchase of fishing supplies and other necessary items. "If we do not supply them with their requirements," said Barker, "either in cash or nets, they will go to our competitors, who are only too anxious to get their services."[17]

Table 12.   Canning Expenses of Columbia River Packers Association, 1917

Item	Cost per case[a]	Percent of total cost
Fish	$ 7.10	55
Cannery labor	1.71	13
Cans	1.58	12
Selling expenses	0.69	5
Depreciation	0.40	1
Boxes and labels	0.35	2
Office expenses	0.28	3
Cannery maintenance	0.26	3
Fish handling	0.19	2
Taxes	0.17	1
Factory insurance	0.13	1
Other (power, fuel, freight, supplies, spoilage, rent)	0.09	1
TOTAL	12.95	
Selling price per case[b]	14.00	
Estimated profit per case	1.05	

SOURCE: Columbia River Packers Association, Barker Papers, Oregon Historical Society, MSS 1699.

[a] Per case of ½-pound flats, 48 pounds to the case.
[b] Opening price per case.

[16] Fred Barker to P. H. McCue, Northwestern Fisheries Company, March 16, 1922 (Portland, Oregon Historical Society), MSS 1699, Box 6.
[17] Fred Barker to T. Chutter, January 25, 1917, and Barker to A. B. Hammond, January 29, 1923 (Portland, Oregon Historical Society), MSS 1699, Box 6.

Keeping fishermen in line was a continual task, and most of the responsibility fell on station managers. Sometimes the cannery manager helped with personnel problems. George H. George wrote one station manager in 1911 after talking with a gillnetter that "he promises to be a good dog hereafter, so we have let him take a boat. We don't think we will have any more trouble with Nick, but for safety's sake," George said, "see that he doesn't take more than one net at a time."[18] On another occasion Barker wrote one of his station managers, "If you see the old man, just stir him up a little. He did very well last year, and he should be doing a great deal better now than he is."[19]

In addition to "stirring up" fishermen, much of the canner's effort was in maintaining rapport with fishers. This was accomplished by many small acts. For example, one such act was getting Nick Stanovich's fine for hoarding flour during World War I reduced to $100. Another was getting government dredges to stop interfering with fishermen. One of the association's station managers also served as clerk for the railroad. He had $155.89 stolen, and the railroad wanted him to pay for the loss. Barker wrote McLeod, "Huycke is a very good man and should he leave us on account of this trouble not being cleared up, he would be a very hard man to replace, that is at the salary we can afford to pay."[20] McLeod contacted the railroad management and settled the matter. Moses Laquet, one of the association's oldest gillnetters, was arrested for carrying passengers for hire without a license. Barker again asked McLeod's help stating that McGowan, our neighbor there, "is of course more or less in competition to get the services of good fishermen."[21] When Ernest Woodfield died in 1921, the association donated $1,500 to his widow to acknowledge Woodfield's contribution as association foreman on the Sand Island seining grounds. There was a question in 1917 as to what settlement a boat

[18] George H. George to Anton Peterson, May 28, 1911 (Portland, Oregon Historical Society), MSS 1699, Box 13.
[19] Fred Barker to J. V. Giaconi, June 20, 1916 (Portland, Oregon Historical Society), MSS 1699, Box 50.
[20] Fred Barker to George B. McLeod, October 26, 1916 (Portland, Oregon Historical Society), MSS 1699, Box 42.
[21] Fred Barker to George B. McLeod, January 8, 1919 (Portland, Oregon Historical Society), MSS 1699, Box 42.

Salmon seining (Weister photo, Oregon Historical Society).

puller should get when the boat captain died. Barker wrote Hammond, "There is a question as to whether the lien that a boat puller might have on any fish caught does not die with him, but we would not want to get any notoriety among the fishermen that would be detrimental to our interests. One of the principal assets of this business is our standing with the fishermen."[22]

Cannery managers were not only protective of their workers, but they identified territories they felt were theirs. In 1920, after the association purchased land near one of his buying stations, F. M. Warren wrote Barker, "We have always hesitated to butt in on what we considered other people's legitimate business simply for the sake of causing trouble." Warren, concerned about the potential competition, wrote, "Frankly, I think that the actions of your company in regards to this are going to mean a very spirited price war."[23]

To meet the needs of fishermen, a store was associated with most of the salmon-buying stations. The store, like all other aspects of the cannery, was to be run at a profit. W. O. Barnes wrote to Cook Cannery station manager in 1911, "Remember when buying groceries and other goods, that goods well bought are goods half sold—that is, if you get in and buy when the market is low and buy when things are cheap, with an eye to selling them later or when they have advanced that there is just as much made that way that there is in buying as you want the goods and paying the prevailing market price for them."[24] On the other hand, the station manager was also admonished for buying too many matches—that could be a fire hazard!

Each fisherman had a book summarizing his purchases, landings, and cash advances. When one of Hammond's accountants wanted to eliminate these books as an economy measure, Barker wrote

[22] Fred Barker to A. B. Hammond, October 11, 1917 (Portland, Oregon Historical Society), MSS 1699, Box 42.
[23] F. M. Warren to Fred Barker, February 4, 1920 (Portland, Oregon Historical Society), MSS 1699, Box 6.

[24] W. O. Barnes to Cook Cannery Station Manager, March 16, 1911 (Portland, Oregon Historical Society), MSS 1699, Box 13.

that the fishermen "look upon the books that we give them in the same light as the ordinary depositor at a bank would a passbook." Barker emphasized, "This business is entirely dependent upon the goodwill of the fishermen, and their confidence in us for fair dealing."[25]

The purchases and cash advances created a bond of debt between the fisher and canner. The bond was carefully monitored. W. O. Barnes alerted one of the station managers in 1911 that two fishermen had just quit to fish for A. Booth's cannery. "We advise you of this," he wrote, "because if they owe you a balance, it is nothing more than your right that you get after them and see that they deliver you fish to settle the account."[26]

Advances tied up capital. In 1912 fishermen were indebted $125,000 to the Columbia River Packers Association. This was regarded as excessive. The high debts were a result of loans made in 1911 for gillnetters to buy power boats and two very bad fishing years in 1912 and 1913. Even so, the unpaid accounts were reduced to $86,438.73 in 1914.[27] The actual losses due to fishermen's debts were small, $2,000 to $3,000 per year. Canners used the fishermen's gear and equipment as collateral. For example, the debts of one trapman were settled with "a bill of sale for all his trap interests in Baker Bay."[28]

Fishermen paid for the credit and services the canneries extended by receiving lower prices for their fish. The fish price received from canners ranged from 10 to 25 percent below that paid by the cash buyers. Canners competed with the cash buyers for fish. Criticizing one of the cash buyers, Barker wrote one of his station managers in 1914 that he "does not furnish any net racks with conveniences to tan nets, no storage for their nets and boats, in fact, puts out no money whatever, simply pays cash for the fish, and you can readily see the class of men who would sell fish to him are those who do not intend to pay their bills with us."[29]

When there was a shortage of fish the canner-cash buyer competition worked to the fishermen's advantage. The result was a price war for fish. Barker wrote Hammond in 1922, "All manner of prices were paid for spring chinook salmon, cash buyers in some cases were paying as high as 16 cents and 17 cents to fishermen right out of their boats on the river." He said, "We settled with the bulk of our fishermen at 10 cents per pound, but we will have to make another settlement before the end of the year to offset higher cash prices that were paid."[30] The year-end bonus was 2 cents per pound.

In 1923, when the cash buyers were raising the fish price in competition with the canneries who made advances to fishermen, Hammond argued for an aggressive approach. He wrote Barker that if the cash buyers pursued their course "of dealing with the fishermen direct, that you will go into the market yourself and pay cash for fish." Hammond continued, "We are in good shape to do business cheap."[31]

o   o   o   o

Profits were the goal of the cannerymen, but the amount of those profits was difficult to find. Most of the companies were owned by individuals or closed groups, and annual corporate reports were not published or distributed widely. During World War I, studies were made in an attempt to assess the profits of the canners. Definitions of the variables used differed and comparisons are difficult.

One index of profit was the net profit per case of salmon packed. A Federal Trade Commission study made these calculations for 1916 and 1917. The two years illustrate the impact of World War I, which dramatically increased the demand for canned salmon in 1917 and 1918. The war demand doubled profits.

[25] Fred Barker to J. B. Hodge, January 15, 1915 (Portland, Oregon Historical Society), MSS 1699, Box 22.

[26] W. O. Barnes to Nick Stanovich, July 13, 1911 (Portland, Oregon Historical Society), MSS 1699, Box 13.

[27] Fred Barker to A. B. Hammond, February 19, 1914, and Hammond to Barker, April 17, 1923 (Portland, Oregon Historical Society), MSS 1699, Box 22.

[28] George H. George to R. A. Hawkins, March 31, 1911 (Portland, Oregon Historical Society), MSS 1699, Box 6.

[29] Fred Barker to Theodore Ospund, May 23, 1914 (Portland, Oregon Historical Society), MSS 1699, Box 23.

[30] Fred Barker to A. B. Hammond, September 25, 1922 (Portland, Oregon Historical Society), MSS 1699, Box 6.

[31] A. B. Hammond to Fred Barker, May 2, 1923 (Portland, Oregon Historical Society), MSS 1699, Box 6.

Net racks furnished by canneries (Oregon Historical Society).

Gillnetters' rendevous near Sand Island buying stations (Oregon Historical Society).

The profits of Columbia River canners were intermediate between those of Alaska and Puget Sound (Table 13). This was because Alaska packed

Table 13. Salmon Canners' Net Profits on Investment, 1916-1917

Area	Profit per case ($)	
	1916	1917
Alaska	$1.30	$2.39
Puget Sound	0.67	1.31
Columbia River	1.10	1.83
AVERAGE	1.10	2.27

SOURCE: Federal Trade Commission, *Canned Foods, Canned Salmon,* (Washington, D.C., 1919), p. 61.

more good grades of salmon than Puget Sound. Good grade salmon commanded higher prices than the poorer grades. Costs of obtaining salmon were lower in Alaska and higher on Puget Sound. On the Columbia River more good grades of salmon were packed, but the cost of obtaining fish was high.

A second profit index is the ratio of gross profits to company assets. Gross profits are the excess of income over costs before deducting for deprecia-

tion. Depreciation was not very carefully calculated prior to 1900, but the income tax laws of 1913 led to more careful consideration of deductions.

Gross profit information for the Columbia Packers Association from 1906 to 1916 was available for five of the eleven years. The average was 6.6 percent. Information was not available for 1913, the only year the association lost money, and for 1915, the best year ever. The 6.6 percent profit figure was comparable to the Alaska Packers Association average of 6.2 percent.[32] Net profits varied from 1 to 4 percentage points less than gross profits.

The war-year profits increased despite price controls. Columbia River canneries showed gross profits of 10 to 15 percent of assets. The profit picture was very good and extra dividends were paid. Canners in the late nineteenth century typically paid 10 percent dividends. Eureka and Epicure, one of the companies incorporated in the Columbia River Packers Association, was paying 28 to 40 percent annual dividends. After consolidation, the association paid regular annual dividends of 6 per-

[32] Columbia River Packers Association papers (Portland, Oregon Historical Society), MSS 1699; and W. O. Barnes papers (Seattle, University of Washington Documents Collections).

cent on stock with a par value of $100. The actual market value in 1915 and 1916 averaged $69. Extra dividends were paid in years when profits were good. During World War I, a 6 percent extra was paid in Liberty Bonds to association stockholders. The postwar depression cut into the canners' profits, and most companies showed losses for brief periods in the early 1920s.

Under Barker's management the association's financial position improved. Debt was reduced and annual dividends were paid regularly. When Hammond sold out his interest in 1923, the company surplus exceeded $1.5 million. Association assets were $3.8 million. The first quarter of the twentieth century had been a success for the association in terms of "hauling in the net."

Chapter 7/

Salmon Cheaper Than Meat

THE INNOVATION to can salmon was dependent on finding consumers for the product. On the first attempts of Hapgood, Hume and Company to market Sacramento River salmon R. D. Hume commented, "The article being new to the merchants of San Francisco, they would have nothing to do with it for a long time."[1] Domestic sales did not provide the consumers required, and in the early 1870s the Humes discovered markets in Great Britain, where canned salmon provided a cheap and nourishing food for the Midland industrial workers. R. D. Hume explained the reason for the European market potential: "For many years prior to the advent of salmon canning on the Pacific Coast, owing to the scarcity of these fish in other parts of the civilized world, salmon had become a luxury item of which none but the wealthy could partake."[2]

Great Britain imported more than 60 percent of the U.S. canned salmon exports from 1900 to 1915. As the major export market, Great Britain was the key to finding markets in other areas at the turn of the century. British Africa took 95 percent of the salmon going to Africa. In Oceania over 90 percent of the canned salmon went to Australia. The British East Indies, primarily India, took 80 percent of the canned salmon exported to Asia. Principal export areas in North America were British Columbia and the British West Indies.[3]

From 1866 to 1885 the number of consumers grew rapidly and demand for canned salmon increased. The number of Columbia River canneries increased from 1 to 39, and the number of fishermen increased from 4 to more than 3,500. The pack grew from 4,000 to 629,000 cases of 48 one-pound cans. Consumers benefited from the competition among canners for their food dollar. Wholesale prices declined from $16 to $4.75 per case. The prices received by fishermen increased from 15 to 75 cents per fish (Appendix B). This was the golden age as fishers, canners, and consumers benefited from commercialization of the salmon resource. Even though average wages and profits declined, those received in the 1880s were considered good.

By the mid-1880s, the market could not take all the salmon, and the *Oregonian* noted that the "working classes of Great Britain have for years steadily become less able to buy the fish, and lessened consumption has consequently played an important part in determining values and controlling demands."[4] R. D. Hume said, "Not much effort was made to create a demand in the United

---

[1] Robert D. Hume, *Salmon of the Pacific Coast* (San Francisco: Schmidt Label & Lithographic Co., 1893), p. 8.
[2] Robert D. Hume, 1893, p. 15 (see note 1).

[3] John N. Cobb, *The Salmon Fisheries of the Pacific Coast*, (Washington, D.C., 1911), Bureau of Fisheries Document No. 751, pp. 140-145.
[4] January 1, 1885.

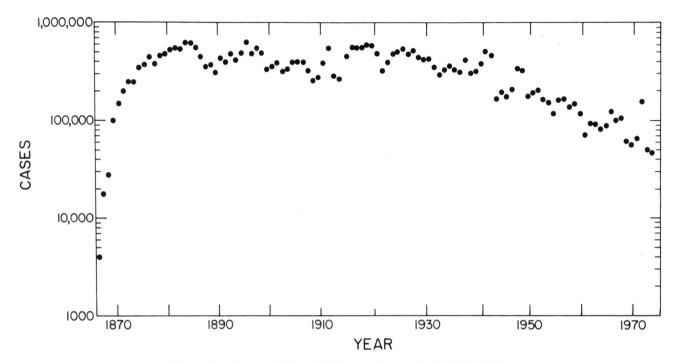

Figure 4.   Cases of Columbia River salmon packed, 1866-1973.

States until the increase of pack had overloaded the other markets."[5]

Too many fishers, too few fish, and too few consumers led to an adjustment after 1885. The number of canneries declined from 39 to 21 by 1889. The number of fishers decreased from 3,500 to less than 3,000, and the pack declined from 600,000 to 310,000 cases (Figure 4). Canners sought new consumers. Completion of the transcontinental railroads opened up eastern markets, and in 1898 the railroad was extended to Astoria.

*   *   *   *

Product quality was one of the factors that attracted consumers. Quality control began with how fishermen handled their catch. During each phase from landing to canning to marketing, the cannery manager was concerned with effects on the consumer. In a memo to station managers, George H. George told them to instruct fishermen "to take as good care as possible of their large fish and keep them covered in the boat so that the sun and wind will not blister them, and when they take them out of the net ask the fishermen to put them in the boat

gently and not throw them down which breaks the grain of meat."[6] Some canners preferred salmon caught by traps because of their better quality. With traps, fish did not have to be taken from the water until ready for packing, and only the amount required for packing needed to be taken. Canners did not have to take poor quality fish, and the pack was made up of only the freshest and best fish.

Canners were careful to pack salmon so that its appearance was pleasing to the consumer. Cans from each batch were tested to check the proper amount of oil and moistness of the fish. Proper color was an important market consideration. Initially, sockeye were difficult to market because of their deep red color. Pink salmon never enjoyed top ratings among consumers because of their pale color. Stanford University professor, David Starr Jordan, summarized the different market qualities of salmon for the *Pacific Fisherman*.[7] He said, "The flesh of the chinook salmon when canned is richer

[5] Robert D. Hume, 1893, p. 16 (see note 1).

[6] George H. George to Andrew Luksich, circa July 1912 (Portland, Oregon Historical Society), MSS 1699, Box 8.

[7] *Pacific Fisherman* 2 (May 1904), p. 25.

Trap-caught fish are not taken from water until ready for packing (Benji Gifford photo, Oregon Historical Society).

in flavor and more agreeable than that of any of the others." The red salmon or sockeye ranked second. "It is firmer, drier, and less attractive than the chinook," wrote Jordan. Silver or coho salmon were paler, but about as good as the red salmon. The pink or humpback salmon had a different flavor and spoiled quicker.

Columbia River canners perceived their product to be best in quality. The prices paid for the various Pacific Coast salmon packs indicated this was true. Columbia River fancy chinook salmon sold at higher prices than Alaska red salmon in every year except 1919 and 1925. Prices for Columbia River chinook were usually 50 percent above prices for pink salmon.

The cannery manager usually marketed canned salmon through a broker. The broker was a salesman, friend, confidential adviser, and sometimes a financial backer. Hapgood, Hume and Company got the money for their cannery supplies from a

San Francisco broker, William T. Coleman. Usually, long-term relations between the cannery manager and broker worked out best. Brokers received a 5 percent commission. During World War I, strong market conditions led many canners who were trying to save commission costs to take over the broker's role themselves. The postwar depression changed this practice. With softening of the market, canners found the market connections and services of a broker very valuable.

The premier position of Columbia River chinook salmon led to conflict among the salmon-canning areas. The *Morning Astorian* for February 29, 1896, carried an article accusing Puget Sound canners of marketing "Dog Fish Labeled Columbia River Salmon." Chum salmon were often referred to as "dog fish." The *Astorian* claimed that the "alleged salmon is one of the vilest classes of fish, and yet the Columbia River chinook salmon is dragged down by this outrage."[8] After World War

I, the government returned much of the salmon it had purchased. Some of it turned out to be of inferior quality. This led to the chiding of one area by another over the quality of their respective products. San Francisco broker, Frank B. Peterson, chided the quality of returned Columbia River salmon in his advertising brochure, stating that it is "in our opinion, as good as it ever has been for the past thirty or forty years."[9] Columbia River canner, F. M. Warren, picked up on this implication of a history of poor quality packing by proposing his own circular slighting the quality of salmon sold by Peterson. Warren proposed, "Frank B. Peterson is offering a lot which was rejected by both British and United States Army inspectors on account of a reported high percentage of taints. We, of course, believe that the inspectors were unfair and that his goods are fully equal to what he has been packing."[10]

*   *   *   *

In addition to the quality of the product, price was believed to be one of the important determinants affecting the number of consumers. A high price brought high profits, yet cannery managers were concerned about the long-term effects of too high a price. "If the housewife, who has so many pennies each day to expend for food, has purchased, for instance, a can of salmon for 12¢, say once or twice each week, and notes the price has advanced to 15¢, she will pass salmon and purchase a substitute."[11] In some situations a lower price for salmon was advantageous. Samuel Elmore pointed out that in 1898, when Alaska red and Columbia River chinook were nearly equal in price, "Consumers of salmon have had an opportunity to compare the genuine Columbia River article with the cheap low grade of fish packed at outside points."[12]

The high quality of Columbia River canned salmon commanded a higher price. Canners, however, were concerned about the relationship between price and quantity. A 1910 article in the *Pacific Fisherman* asked, "How long will salmon be a staple?" It noted, "So far as the mere question of supply and demand is concerned, the situation this year and last warranted a much higher price than was established, but salmon packers realized that too large an advance would put the retail price of salmon to a point where it would become a fancy food article."[13]

Canners also felt that a stable price was better than one that fluctuated a great deal. George H. George wrote to Hammond in 1912 about demand for Alaska red salmon, "The prices on this grade last year were too high, and resulted in stopping consumption." George went on to say about prices, "It would be much better to carry them along on a uniform basis, where the consumption would be stimulated and kept moving, than to inflate prices beyond this point with a view of making a good big clean-up one year, and pay for it the next."[14]

The low packs of 1912 and 1913 could not fill the orders of brokers. At this time Columbia River canners were able to deliver only 60 percent of their orders. Fred Barker complained to Hammond in 1914, "The great trouble with this business is not in selling our salmon, but in getting the salmon to pack."[15] The problem was short-lived. In the summer of 1915, Barker wrote his brother Will, "We have enough salmon to supply our regular trade in the country if we do not pack any Columbia River chinooks for two years to come."[16] Holding prices when there was an oversupply became a game of bluffing to cover a weak hand. When brokers learned of the good runs in 1914 and 1915, they began to ask when prices would be reduced.

[8] *Morning Astorian*, February 29, 1896, p. 1.
[9] Frank B. Peterson, Circular 84, June 2, 1919 (Portland, Oregon Historical Society), MSS 1699, Box 6.
[10] F. M. Warren to Frank B. Peterson, June 12, 1919 (Portland, Oregon Historical Society), MSS 1699, Box 6.
[11] *Morning Astorian*, March 11, 1916.
[12] *Weekly Astorian*, March 3, 1898, p. 4.

[13] *Pacific Fisherman* 8 (August 1910), p. 15.
[14] George H. George to A. B. Hammond, October 3, 1912 (Portland, Oregon Historical Society), MSS 1699, Box 5.
[15] Fred Barker to A. B. Hammond, May 7, 1914 (Portland, Oregon Historical Society), MSS 1699, Box 5.
[16] Fred Barker to William H. Barker, September 28, 1915 (Portland, Oregon Historical Society), MSS 1699, Box 5.

"Every pound of food taken from the sea relieves the land of producing a corresponding amount of meat." (Quoted from *Harper's Weekly*, November 1, 1913, p. 6; photo from Oregon Historical Society).

Barker responded that "it was the packer's intention to raise prices after September 1st, on account of the short pack of first grade salmon elsewhere." At the same time, he told his brother Will, then president of the British Columbia Packers Association, that he realized "it would be the worst thing we could do to give the jobbers any inkling as to our anxiety to sell our first grade chinooks."[17]

The reason for the abrupt change in the pack was vastly increased salmon runs. Only 27 million pounds were caught on the Columbia in 1912 and 1913. In 1914 and 1915 the total catch was 43 million pounds.[18] The increase in pack was attributed to the hatchery program. Barker wrote McLeod in 1915, favoring retention of Oregon's Master Fish Warden, R. E. Clanton: "While we do not put it out to the trade or give it publicity, yet our pack this year is far ahead of even 1914 up to date." Both years, according to Barker, showed "very good results for hatchery work."[19]

Pacific Coast salmon production grew rapidly. From three million cases in 1900, the pack doubled by 1912. Salmon canning was even tried in Siberia. Japanese canning companies sold salmon canned in Siberia to world markets in 1910. Siberian canneries were not expected to compete with domestic canned salmon because "development of the fisheries has been greatly retarded by the Russians, who, while lacking practical knowledge of how best to prosecute the fisheries, and also lacking the capital necessary to finance them, yet are not willing to allow foreigners to exploit them."[20] The most common Siberian salmon species were the pink and chum salmon, which were regarded as a low grade for packing. Salting of salmon was more important than canning in Siberia. Despite these dire predictions, the salmon packed in Siberia grew to 10 percent of the North American salmon pack by 1927. Alaska, however, was the area with the great-

est production and most rapid growth. From 1.5 million cases in 1900, the Alaska pack increased to 3.7 million cases in 1913. Salmon canning expanded to Japan that year, and for the first time the North Pacific salmon pack reached 8 million cases, or more than 300 million pounds.

To market the increased salmon pack, canners formed organizations to promote their product, much like what had been done in the canned pineapple industry. One of the promotions was a National Canned Salmon Day. The first one was held on March 14, 1913, timed to coincide with the beginning of the Lenten season.

The promotion efforts of canners were aided by several government agencies. Several 1913 issues of *Harper's Magazine* carried articles on the U.S. Bureau of Chemistry and its newly appointed director, Dr. Carl L. Alsberg. Having just completed three years on special assignment with the Bureau of Fisheries, Alsberg was convinced that "every pound of food taken from the sea relieves the land of producing a corresponding amount of meat."[21] A U.S. Department of Agriculture bulletin showed the price of canned pink salmon was less than 10 cents per pound.[22] Chicken, lamb, beef, veal, and pork cost twice as much. The U.S. Bureau of Fisheries summed it up with a circular entitled, *Canned Salmon: Cheaper Than Meats and Why.*[23] The circular's title emphasized that to attract consumers canned salmon had to compete with other commonly used food items.

✿   ✿   ✿   ✿

World War I, however, had a far greater impact than the promotion efforts of the canners and the government. The war created increased demands for canned salmon. Exports doubled and the salmon pack increased by one-third. Sales to Europe increased two and a half times to an average annual domestic export of more than 80 mil-

[17] Fred Barker to William H. Barker, August 29, 1915 (Portland, Oregon Historical Society), MSS 1699, Box 5.

[18] Joseph A. Craig and Robert L. Hacker, "The History and Development of the Fisheries of the Columbia River," *Bulletin of the Bureau of Fisheries* 49 (1940), p. 201.

[19] Fred Barker to George B. McLeod, June 9, 1915 (Portland, Oregon Historical Society), MSS 1699, Box 42.

[20] *Pacific Fisherman Yearbook* 13 (1915), p. 66.

[21] *Harper's Magazine*, October 25, 1913, p. 6.

[22] *Pacific Fisherman* 10 (October 1912), p. 21, gives facts taken from Department of Agriculture Bulletin 142.

[23] *Pacific Fisherman* 12 (April 1914), p. 11, makes reference to printing of 100,000 copies of *Canned Salmon: Cheaper Than Meats and Why*, Bureau of Fisheries Economic Circular No. 11.

lion pounds. The U.S. government added to the canned salmon demand by purchasing over half the Alaska pack. Increased foreign and domestic demand led to sharply higher prices. Columbia River canned salmon prices advanced over 50 percent between 1916 and 1917. Comparable price increases occurred in the other salmon-producing areas.

The war conditioned consumers to higher salmon prices. Figure 5 shows wholesale salmon prices, standardized to 1957-1959 dollars, plotted against the quantity sold. The wholesale price for each grade of salmon packed in each area was called the "opening price." This was the price canners set for their product. Usually it was not set until well into the season. The opening price was based on the expected local pack, the pack in outside areas, the quantity unsold from the previous year, and general economic conditions. Large or small packs in Alaska, Puget Sound, or British Columbia could affect the Columbia River opening price. Every attempt was made by canners to hold

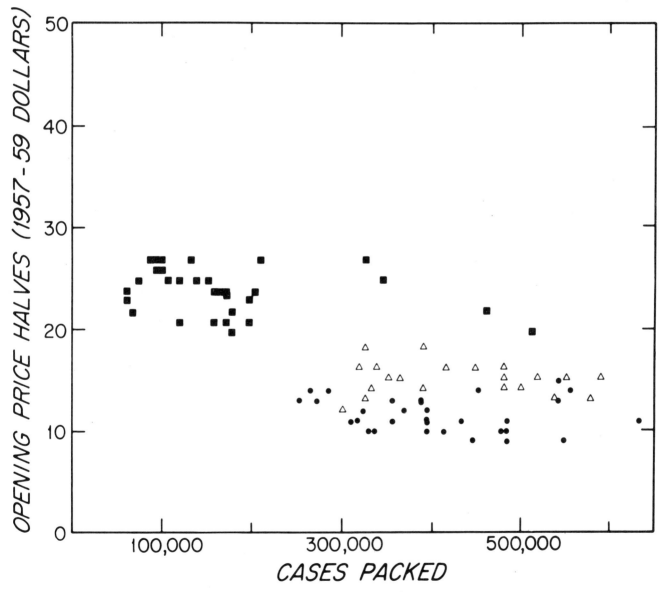

Figure 5.   Pricing patterns for Columbia River canned salmon, standardized to 1957-1959 dollars. ■ = 1942-1973, △ = 1917-1941, ● = 1886-1916

Putting salmon in cans, Astoria (Oregon Historical Society).

the opening price. When faced with an oversupply in 1915, Barker remarked, "Warren and one or two others have advocated a further reduction in price, but we have held them down, and hope that there will be no breaking of prices from now on."[24] While the opening price is not a perfect index, it is "the most satisfactory basis for showing price trends over a long period of time."[25] To correct for the effects of inflation and make real dollar comparisons in the prices for Columbia River canned salmon, open prices used in Figure 5 are standardized to 1957-1959 dollars. The figure and Table 14 show the dual impacts of the canners' desire to hold prices constant irrespective of the quantity which could be sold and the new price levels created by World Wars I and II.

[24] Fred Barker to A. B. Hammond, July 15, 1915 (Portland, Oregon Historical Society), MSS 1699, Box 5.
[25] Daniel B. DeLoach, *The Salmon Canning Industry*, (Corvallis, Oregon State College, 1939), p. 101.

Table 14. Opening Price and Quantity Relationships for Columbia River Salmon

Period	Slope, K[a]	Significance (F test)
1866-1885	4.79	0.001
1886-1916	0.47	n.s.
1917-1940	0.38	n.s.
1941-1971[b]	2.13	n.s.

SOURCE: Appendix B.

[a] The equation Log Q = Log C–K (Log P) is used to calculate K. Q is cases packed, C is a constant, and P is opening price of fancy chinook. When K is above 1.0, supply is inelastic. When K is below 1.0, supply is more elastic.
[b] Price data not reported after 1971.

During the initial period of commercialization, 1866 to 1885, salmon production increased and prices to consumers decreased (Figure 6). The quantity of salmon supplied was very responsive to price. This is shown in the value of K, which is much greater than 1.0. The reverse was true for

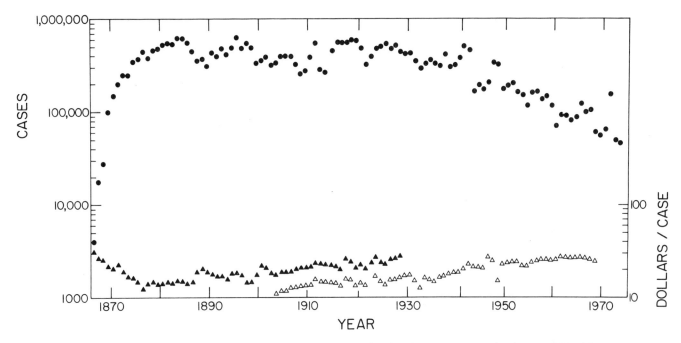

Figure 6. Cases packed and opening price (1957-1959 dollars) of Columbia River canned salmon, 1866-1973. ● = cases packed, ▲ = opening price talls, △ = opening price halves

the 1886-1916 and 1917-1940 periods. The salmon price did not vary with the pack size in any patterned way. During each of these periods canners held prices relatively constant irrespective of the quantity which could be sold. What seemed more important was canned salmon's competitive position relative to other commonly used food items. The value of K below 1.0 reflects this situation in which supply is very elastic (quite variable) while price remains relatively constant.

Each war raised the price level at which canned salmon was held. Figure 6 shows that from 1886 to 1916, the period preceding World War I, standardized opening prices for Columbia River salmon averaged around $12 per case (1957-1959 dollars). In 1917, World War I caused a dramatic increase in demand for canned salmon and opening prices increased a step. Between World War I and World War II, the standardized opening price averaged $15.60 per case (1957-1959 dollars).

There were short-term fluctuations in price involving the quantity of canned salmon available. For example, when the government returned much of the salmon it had purchased during World War I, a brief depression occurred in the salmon market. The 1920 prices for Columbia River canned salmon

were the best ever because of a short pack in Alaska. The next spring brokers warned that they had "heavy stocks and it will not be their intention to buy ahead this year; . . . therefore, it is advisable for every packer to be conservative and only pack the earliest and best fish and get the market back in shape again for another year."[26] The Great Depression of the 1930s reduced the quantity of Columbia River salmon packed. In 1932 less than 300,000 cases were packed and the wholesale price was at pre-World War I levels. During the 1930s, large quantities of foreign fish products were imported into the United States, competing with domestic products. Also, during the 1930s, salmon spawning habitat along the Columbia River was lost to other uses and salmon production declined.

Market studies show that despite the postwar depression, the Great Depression, and the loss of habitat, canned salmon continued to be cheaper than meat in the 1930s. In 1934, red salmon was 21 cents and sirloin steak was 31 cents per pound.[27]

[26] H. L. North to S. S. Gordon, March 30, 1921 (Portland, Oregon Historical Society), MSS 1699, Box 6.

[27] Pacific American Fisheries, Inc., *A Review of the Salmon Industry with Particular Reference to Pacific American Fisheries, Inc.* (Seattle, 1935), p. 5.

Canned salmon provided two to four times as much protein per dollar as eggs, lamb, chicken, sirloin steak, or ham. Canned salmon continued to compete for the consumer's basic food dollar and to supply day-to-day requirements.

The effects of World War II on the salmon market were similar to those of World War I. Between 1941 and 1942, Columbia River canned salmon prices advanced 25 percent to a standardized price of $24.50 (1957-1959 dollars) that held through 1971. At this price, salmon was no longer cheaper than meat. Canned salmon was now more expensive than the basic foods purchased by consumers to meet their day-to-day needs.

On a 1957 tour, British Columbia salmon broker, Harold G. Haggart, visited salmon markets in all areas of the world. He found that "everybody likes canned salmon, but nobody likes the price."[28] The number of potential consumers far exceeded the supply, and Haggart reported that canned salmon was "in high favor as a luxury item" in all countries he visited.

In the 1960s, the canning of salmon from Oregon and Washington coastal streams was largely discontinued. The salmon caught there were sold fresh or frozen to tourists and to luxury consumers in restaurants and specialty food stores. Columbia River canneries continued to can salmon, but from 1962 to 1973 canned salmon decreased from 72 to 25 percent of the commercial catch. By 1975 most of the canning lines were closed. Canned salmon was no longer a basic item in the food budgets of industrial workers. Cheaper food had taken its place. The post-World War II price increase put canned salmon beyond the reach of average consumers. Canned salmon had become, as the 1910 *Pacific Fisherman* had feared, "a fancy food article."

[28] *Pacific Fisherman* 55 (October 1957), p. 50.

Chapter 8/

Loss of Habitat

JUST EIGHT YEARS after Hapgood, Hume and Company opened their salmon cannery on the Sacramento River, efforts were begun there to artificially rear salmon. The purpose was not to improve the supplies in the Sacramento, but to obtain eggs at a lower cost for planting in Atlantic Coast salmon streams.

At a June 13, 1872, meeting of hatcherymen in Boston, Livingston Stone suggested the Pacific Coast as a source for salmon eggs. Stone had four years of experience with a New Hampshire Fish Commission project to restore salmon in local rivers. The goal of obtaining Pacific Coast salmon eggs was to secure fish which would "give sport to the angler."[1] Supplies of *Salmo salar,* the Atlantic salmon, from Canada had become too difficult to obtain, and local supplies were not available in sufficient quantities. The people of New Brunswick had become very hostile to people from the United States taking their salmon eggs, and Canada was charging $40 per 1,000 eggs. Since millions of eggs were required, this was too expensive.

With an appropriation of $5,000, Stone started a hatchery on the McCloud River, a tributary to the Sacramento, in the fall of 1872. The first year only 30,000 eggs were shipped east. The cost was $100 per thousand.[2] Stone, however, proved that shipping Pacific Coast eggs east by rail was possible, and by 1875 costs were down to 50 cents per thousand. Eggs from the McCloud hatchery were also shipped to Europe, Australia, New Zealand, and 27 states including the land-bound states of Colorado, Utah, Iowa, Kansas, and the Great Lakes states.

Some people believed all Northeastern rivers would have abundant salmon runs. Because the eggs came from California, people felt that salmon runs could be started in warmer, southern Atlantic Coast rivers that had never had Atlantic salmon. The young Pacific Coast fry developed rapidly in their new environments. Vast numbers of them were observed going down to the sea, but what became of them was an "unfathomable mystery. Except in very rare isolated instances, these young salmon were never seen again!"[3]

Actually, the transplant of shad and striped bass from the East Coast to San Francisco Bay in 1871 was much more successful. By 1903, fishers on the Columbia River reported, "There are so many shad in the river and being caught in traps and seines that they have not only become a drug on the market, but are a nuisance."[4]

[1] Spencer F. Baird, "Reports of Special Conferences with American Fish-Culturists' Association and State Commissioners of Fisheries," *Report of the Commissioner of Fish and Fisheries for 1872-73* (Washington, D.C., 1874), p. 758.

[2] Livingston Stone, "The Artificial Propagation of Salmon on the Pacific Coast of the United States," *Bulletin of the Fish Commission* 16 (1897), p. 206.

[3] Stone, 1896, p. 219 (see note 2).

[4] *Pacific Fisherman* 1 (May 1903), p. 9.

Stone's efforts at the McCloud hatchery demonstrated that hatcheries could restore runs in a
river. The McCloud hatchery closed in 1883 because of a river obstruction 8 miles downstream
that prevented salmon migration upstream. The
hatchery was reopened in 1888. That year Sacramento River landings began a precipitous decline.
Landings exceeded 4 million pounds in 1888 and
reached a low of 170,245 pounds in 1891. Landings
increased to 1.5 million pounds in 1892, four years
after reopening the hatchery and the first year that
results from the hatchery work could be expected.
The increase in catch to 2.5 million pounds in 1895
was credited to the McCloud hatchery.[5]

✳   ✳   ✳   ✳

The fact that hatcheries were necessary to
maintain salmon runs was recognized early on the
Columbia River. An 1876 newspaper article said,
"It is really wonderful that with all the catch of late
years, the supply has not shown perceptible decrease; but the history of eastern rivers assures us
that the end will come unless artificial means are
adopted to assist propagation."[6] Columbia River
cannerymen organized the Oregon and Washington Fish Propagation Company in 1873, and in
1877 they hired Livingston Stone to build a hatchery on the Clackamas River. The Clackamas hatchery was never too successful, being "too near civilization . . . and gradually mills and dams, timber-
cutting on the upper waters of the Clackamas, and
logging in the river, together with other adverse
influences crippled its efficiency."[7]

Hatchery work was not well supported in the
1880s. There was the token effort by canners. Canneryman R. D. Hume was the most innovative
hatcheryman of the time. After observing the
McCloud hatchery, he opened one in 1877, the
first year he established operations on the Rogue
River. He conducted several experiments to determine the proper methods for hatching salmon.
He later argued that his pack was a result of his
hatchery work four years earlier. The years for
which Hume predicted better catches resulting

from hatchery releases showed an average production 40 percent greater than the non-hatchery
years.[8]

Even though the Clackamas hatchery had little
apparent impact on the Columbia, it demonstrated
a willingness to pursue hatchery development. Ex-
tensive hatchery developments were begun on the
Columbia in the 1890s. At this time Washington,
Oregon, and the federal government began artificial propagation on a significant scale. Between
1895 and 1900 hatchery production tripled to a release of over 23 million eggs and fry. Hatchery
production nearly tripled again by 1905 to 62 million eggs and fry.[9]

Evidence of the effects of this expanded hatchery effort came from the August 1903 *Pacific
Fisherman*, which reported a late July-early August
run of a "magnitude never before equalled." This
run recurred in 1904, changing outlooks for a dis-
appointing pack. The new run was of short dura-
tion and could be packed only "if sufficient preparation is made to handle it in a few weeks time
instead of a long drawn out time as in the past."[10]
Comment in 1905 on the new run of fish was:
"There seems no question but that 75 percent of
the salmon entering the river are directly attributable to artificial propagation."[11]

Despite this apparent success, the Columbia
River salmon and steelhead landings declined from
nearly 38 million pounds in 1905 to 24 million
pounds in 1909. Hatcherymen were concerned
about the apparent gap between their efforts and
the results. Through the early 1900s they had ex-
perimented with systems of ponding salmon until
they had grown to the fingerling or yearling stage.
At this stage of development, the salmon were better able to survive in the hostile river environment.
Fishermen and cannerymen saw these experiments
as a foolish waste of their hatchery money, but
Oregon Master Fish Warden, Carl D. Shoemaker,

[5] Stone, 1896, p. 229 (see note 2).
[6] See Scrapbook 226b (Portland, Oregon Historical
Society), p. 55.
[7] Stone, 1896, p. 218 (see note 2).

[8] Calculated from Gordon B. Dodds, *The Salmon King
of Oregon, R. D. Hume and the Pacific Fisheries* (Chapel
Hill: University of North Carolina Press, 1959), pp. 238-
239, 131-157.
[9] John N. Cobb, *Pacific Salmon Fisheries*, (Washington, D.C., 1930), Bureau of Fisheries Document No. 1092,
p. 664.
[10] *Pacific Fisherman* 2 (August 1904), p. 8.
[11] *Pacific Fisherman* 3 (August 1905), p. 20.

Fish Commission of Oregon hatchery, Ontario, 1902 (Oregon Historical Society).

argued that the increase in the salmon pack from 266,000 cases in 1913 to 454,000 cases in 1914 resulted from the return of salmon released from ponds in 1910. He said, "The fool idea of four years before had become the savior of the industry because the river was teeming with splendid spring chinooks."[12]

The hatchery effort on the Columbia River augmented the fall chinook runs. Many fall chinook spawned in the lower river and downstream tributaries. In the 1890s fall chinook, because they lacked oil and had less color, were scorned by canners, who expressed hope that little propagation effort would center on these poorer fish.[13] As the spring and summer chinook runs diminished, greater and greater fishing effort was placed on the fall runs. To more fully utilize the fall run, the 1905 salmon season was extended from August 10 to August 25. In the 1880s, most of the canneries closed in late July. An 1894 study showed that chinook salmon "are taken in greatest numbers

about June 10 or 20 of each year."[14] With the hatchery work, the season's peak shifted from mid-June to early August.

An index of the increasing importance of the fall chinook run is the percentage of the run utilized by the cannerymen. In 1892 about 5 percent of the total catch was fall chinook, increasing to 25 percent by 1912 and to 50 percent in 1919-1920. For the 1969-1973 period, fall chinook made up more than half of the commercial salmon catch.[15]

The hatcherymen were proud of their success. In 1910 they formed the Pacific Coast Hatcherymen's Association. At their meeting they chided the scientists: "We have had the opinions of all the scientists with regard to the Pacific coast salmon fisheries, and as time went by their opinions and

[12] Carl D. Shoemaker, "Salmon Hatching Methods," *Oregon Voter* 23 (October 23, 1920), p. 15.

[13] Hugh M. Smith, "Notes on a Reconnaissance of the Fisheries of the Pacific Coast of the United States in 1894," *Bulletin of the Fish Commission* 14 (1895), p. 272.

[14] Smith, 1895, p. 258 (see note 13).

[15] Smith, 1895, p. 242 (see note 13); Willis H. Rich, "The Salmon Runs of the Columbia River in 1938," *Fishery Bulletin of the Fish and Wildlife Service* 50 (1942); Victor E. Smith, "The Taking of Immature Salmon in the Waters of the State of Washington," *Annual Report of the State Fish Commissioner* (Olympia, 1921); and Fish Commission of Oregon and Washington Department of Fisheries, *Status Report, Columbia River Fish Runs and Commercial Fisheries, 1938-70, 1974 Addendum* (Portland, 1975).

Men removing the eggs from female salmon, Ontario hatchery, 1902 (Oregon Historical Society).

their theories were found to be incorrect." The hatcherymen noted that "years of experience and practical study of the habits of the salmon after entering fresh water is certainly of far greater value to the public at large than is the opinion of some scientist who never had the real practical experience year in and year out."[16] John M. Crawford, superintendent of hatcheries for the state of Washington, confidently stated in 1911: "This year's run of salmon on the Columbia River proves beyond a doubt that there is absolutely no real reason for the eventual depletion of the stream by overfishing or the advance of civilization."[17]

＊   ＊   ＊   ＊

The 1920s, however, brought a new threat to the salmon resource. Perhaps hatcheries could correct the problems caused by overfishing, but what about the problem of hydroelectric power

dams on the mainstream of the Columbia? Several writers and fisheries experts have sounded the alarm about the detrimental impacts of Columbia River dams. One of the first voices was Hugh Smith of the U.S. Fish Commission. In an 1894 report he wrote that a dam on the Clackamas River was "one of the greatest evils affecting fisheries of the Columbia Basin."[18] Since then, numerous studies and a variety of popular books and articles have highlighted problems caused by dam construction.[19]

[18] Smith, 1895, p. 244 (see note 13).
[19] Oral Bullard, *Crisis on the Columbia* (Portland: Touchstone Press, 1968); Don Holm, "Where Rolls the Columbia," *Northwest Magazine* (July 20, 1975), pp. 5-21; Steve Lowell, "The Tragedy of the Columbia River," *National Fisherman Yearbook* (1972), pp. 18-21; Anthony Netboy, "Where Have All the Salmon Gone?" *Oregon Times* (July/August 1975), pp. 12-16; Anthony Netboy, *The Salmon: Their Fight for Survival* (Boston: Houghton Mifflin, 1974), pp. 263-310; and Anthony Netboy, *Salmon of the Pacific Northwest: Fish vs. Dams* (Portland: Binfords and Mort, 1958).

[16] *Pacific Fisherman* 8 (May 1910), p. 15.
[17] *Pacific Fisherman* 9 (November 1911), p. 11.

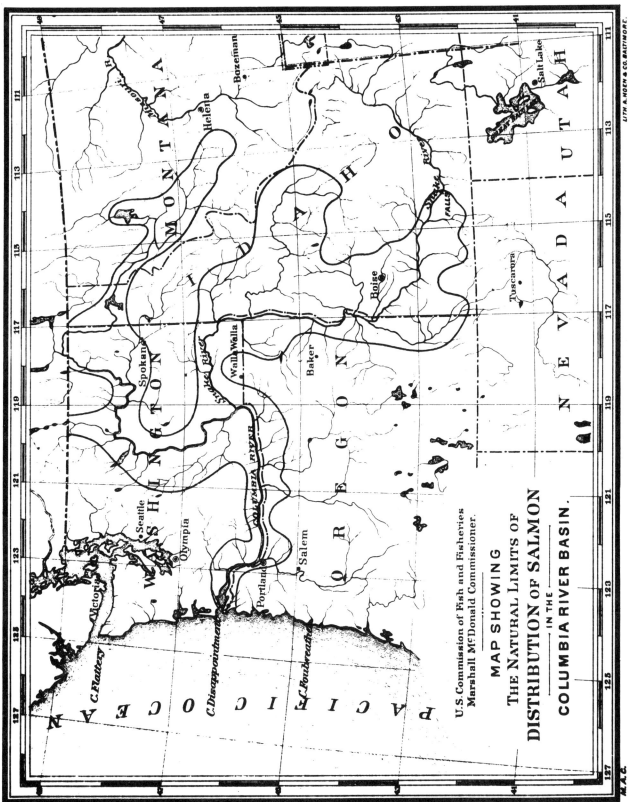

The natural limits of distribution of salmon in the Columbia River, 1892 ("The Salmon Fisheries of the Columbia River Basin," *Bulletin of the Fish Commission*, 1894).

The first mainstream dam, Rock Island, was constructed by the Washington Electric Company. Rock Island Dam is located near Wenatchee, Washington, and was completed in 1933. That same year construction began on Bonneville Dam, just 145 miles from the mouth of the Columbia River. Bonneville Dam was completed in 1938. Grand Coulee, nearly 600 miles upstream, was the next major mainstream dam, completed in 1941. It was built without fish ladders and closed 40 percent of the Columbia River watershed to salmon migration. In 1939, salmon bound for these upper reaches of the Columbia were trapped at Rock Island Dam and transported above Grand Coulee. Roosevelt Lake behind Grand Coulee Dam also destroyed salmon habitat. Attempts were made to relocate the upper Columbia River runs into the Okanogan and Wenatchee river systems.

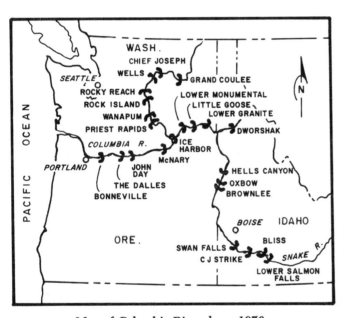

Map of Columbia River dams, 1976.

Dam construction stopped during World War II, but accelerated again with the Korean War. Cold War national security needs dictated that lower river dams be constructed ahead of upper river dams, which would have been less injurious to fish populations. During the 1950s, six dams were started or completed on the Columbia below Grand Coulee and there were four on the Snake.

Dams were not all bad. Livingston Stone found that the only way to capture and hold salmon for spawning was by use of a dam. The fishways associated with some dams acted in the same way as the falls did for the Indians—they concentrated the fish. In 1915, 28 whites and 27 Indians trying to take advantage of this situation were arrested for fishing in the fishway of Prosser Dam on the Yakima River.[20]

To commercial fishers, recreation anglers, and fishery managers, dams were the chief menace facing the salmon populations, and they demanded mitigation. Through 1975, $400 million in federal, state, and private funds were spent on mitigation. Expenditures were "primarily for passage facilities at the dams, although relatively minor amounts were also included for hatcheries, spawning channels, and other forms of mitigation associated with dam construction."[21] Fish passage facilities received $269 million in capital expenditures.[22]

The expenditures on passage facilities represented 6.5 percent of the total capital outlay for major Columbia River structures, but this did not provide for adequate fish passage facilities. Each dam is estimated to cause a 15 percent mortality of downstream migrants.[23] Nitrogen supersaturation is the primary cause. On some runs of juvenile salmon, total mortality is 95 percent. With more dams, excess nitrogen levels since 1965 have reached 135 percent saturation, "well above critical thresholds for both adult and juvenile salmon and steelhead."[24]

Dams were not the only factor causing the loss of salmon habitat. Associated with dams were irrigation projects. Many salmon migrating downstream were diverted into the irrigation canals and ended up on farmers' fields. Dennis Winn, a hatcheryman, was sent to investigate Yakima River salmon losses in Central Washington irrigation

[20] *Pacific Fisherman* 13 (June 1915), p. 15.
[21] Jack Arthur Richards, "An Economic Evaluation of Columbia River Anadromous Fish Programs." Ph.D. thesis, Department of Agricultural Economics, Oregon State University, 1968, p. 18.
[22] Ed Chaney and L. Edward Perry, *Columbia Basin Salmon and Steelhead Analysis* (Portland, Pacific Northwest Regional Commission, 1976), p. 61.
[23] Chaney and Perry, 1976, p. 7 (see note 22).
[24] Chaney and Perry, 1976, p. 6 (see note 22).

ditches in 1916. He found that in July when the salmon were migrating "it is estimated that from 90 to 97 percent of the river passes into irrigation ditches." Winn counted 20 fish per acre, 90 percent of which were migrating juvenile salmon.[25] Recognizing the problem before 1910, the Oregon Legislature passed a law prohibiting unscreened irrigation ditches, but in an attempt to amend the law, "the legislature repealed it."[26] A study by the Fish Commission of Oregon showed that by 1933 dams for irrigation and power on the tributaries to the Columbia had taken "approximately 50 percent of the most important salmon producing area within the basin."[27]

Hatcheries were provided to replace this loss of natural production. They did not receive the same support as fish passage facilities for two reasons. First, hatchery fish were not the same as natural runs in the minds of recreation anglers, nor did hatcheries adequately replace the lost production in the minds of commercial fishers and fishery managers. At best, hatcheries were only partial compensation.

The second reason was that, despite claims to the contrary by hatcherymen, scientists had difficulty proving the value of hatcheries. In 1922, Willis H. Rich wrote, "In the early days . . . the hatcheries probably inflicted as much, or more, damage to the salmon runs as they did service of value."[28] This was because salmon were released with the yolk sac still attached and were highly susceptible to disease and predation. This problem was partially corrected by the use of holding ponds. Through the 1930s, however, hatchery results continued to be inconclusive. British Columbia discontinued its hatchery effort. After World War II, Columbia Basin hatchery production actually declined.[29] In 1952 biologists found tuberculosis among salmon at the Bonneville hatchery.[30] This and other problems with disease transmission led to questions on hatchery effectiveness. Perhaps the hatchery was only serving as a breeding ground for infectious diseases that increased mortality rates.

Completion of Bonneville Dam in 1938 enabled quantitative analysis of the status of Columbia River fish runs. Through the 1940s evidence from the counts at Bonneville showed that some of the salmon runs were in jeopardy. These observations, coupled with a declining salmon pack, led to the initiation of a fisheries development program in 1949. Improvements were begun in the 1950s. Hatchery construction to mitigate losses was a major part of the program. Expenditures on 21 hatcheries, 86 fish ladders over natural barriers, removal of logjams, and restoration of spawning habitats totaled $84 million to 1975.[31] Hatchery production was improved with development of the Oregon Moist Pellet, used extensively after 1959. With this feed, juvenile salmon were inoculated against disease. Economic analysis showed benefit-cost ratios from the mitigation program after 1965 were 1.6 to 1.[32]

Because decline was the problem which the mitigation program was to correct, then what was the trend in run sizes? Six important runs were fished—spring, summer, and fall chinook, blueback, coho, and summer steelhead. Because the enhancement program first received funds in 1949, results could not be expected before 1953. Each of the six runs was analyzed for two periods, 1938-1952 and 1953-1973, to determine run size trends (Table 15).

In the period before the rehabilitation program, summer and fall chinook salmon runs and summer steelhead runs showed a decline (Table 15).

[25] *Pacific Fisherman* 18 (February 1920), p. 25.

[26] H. C. McAllister and R. E. Clanton, *Biennial Report of the Department of Fisheries of the State of Oregon to the Twenty-sixth Legislative Assembly* (Salem, 1911), p. 128.

[27] Fish Commission of Oregon, *Biennial Report to the Thirty-sixth Legislative Assembly* (Salem, 1933), p. 15.

[28] Willis H. Rich, "Early History and Seaward Migration of Chinook Salmon in the Columbia and Sacramento Rivers," *Bulletin of the Bureau of Fisheries* 37 (1922), p. 68.

[29] Jack M. van Hyning, "Factors Affecting the Abundance of Fall Chinook Salmon in the Columbia River," Ph.D. thesis, Department of Fisheries and Wildlife, Oregon State University, 1968, pp. 121-125.

[30] James W. Wood and Erling J. Ordal, "Tuberculosis in Pacific Salmon and Steelhead Trout," *Oregon Fish Commission Contribution No. 25* (1958).

[31] Chaney and Perry, 1976, p. 5 (see note 22).

[32] Richards, 1968, p. 212 (see note 21).

Table 15.   Columbia River Run Size Changes

	Change in no. of fish per year	
Run	1938-1952	1953-1973
Spring chinook	+7,100*	0
Summer chinook	-3,100	-4,900*
Fall chinook	-21,000	+11,500*
Blueback	+5,300	-7,500
Summer steelhead	-3,400	-5,200*
Coho[a]		+37,600

SOURCE: Fish Commission of Oregon and Washington Department of Fisheries, *Status Report, Columbia River Fish Runs and Commercial Fisheries, 1938-1970, 1974 Addendum* (Portland, 1975).

* Calculated using simple linear regression analysis, slope significant at 0.05 or better.
[a] Data available only from 1960-1973.

Spring chinook and blueback runs actually showed an increase. During the rehabilitation the spring chinook run showed no change, while the summer chinook, blueback, and summer steelhead runs continued to decline. The only runs showing significant improvement were the fall chinook and coho runs. The improvement of the coho run was especially dramatic after 1960.

The status of the runs from 1938 to 1973 tells only part of the story. What was the potential catch for Columbia River salmon and steelhead? No records were kept of run size prior to 1938. Assuming that landings bear a close relationship to run size, total landings of Columbia River salmon and steelhead could be an indicator of catch levels and potentials.

Columbia River landings have not, however, been consistently measured. Prior to about 1934, landings were estimated from the quantity of canned, mild-cured, and frozen salmon sold. As long as the pack for these sales came from salmon and steelhead landed on the Columbia, the estimate of landings from sales is acceptable. Francis Seufert, however, brought small amounts of salmon from the Umpqua River in the early 1900s for packing at his plant near The Dalles. The Columbia River Packers Association also purchased salmon from coastal streams. The ratio of salmon packed to landings from 1937 to 1942 indicates significant imports from outside rivers. Evidence for significant outside inputs, however, was un-

available before 1934. The merger of pre-1934 data (based on landings estimated from quantities marketed) with post-1934 data provides a reasonable estimate of quantities landed. These data are plotted in Figure 7.

Figure 7 shows three levels of production— 1880 to 1930, 1931 to 1948, and 1949 to 1973. From 1880 to 1930, the average yield was 33.9 million pounds. There was no distinct growth pattern, although catches varied from a low of 24 to a high of 49 million pounds. In the 1931-1948 period, the average catch declined to 23.8 million, at a rate of 294,000 pounds per year.

What caused the decline in catch from 33.9 to 23.8 million pounds? Government studies in the early 1940s pointed to loss of habitat. "This committee found the startling and deplorable fact that no Columbia tributary above Bonneville Dam, in that portion of the river where the spring chinooks spawn, was in its original natural state." The committee listed eight depletion factors: barrier dams, unscreened diversions, mining barriers, pollution, loss of sufficient water flow, lethal temperatures, loss of natural foods, and overfishing. The economic evaluation of the high dams was criticized as "obviously incorrect until the loss of fish by them is subtracted from their evaluation." The Black Canyon irrigation and power project in Idaho, constructed by the U.S. Bureau of Reclamation in 1924, was blamed for killing off "more thoroughly than all commercial and sports fisheries combined have ever been able to do, the runs of chinook salmon."[33]

Further decline in the Columbia River salmon catches occurred from 1949 to 1973. The average catch dropped to 10.9 million pounds, a decline of more than half the 1931-1948 average. Overall, the 1949-1973 catch indicates no trend, although the curve dips to a low point of only 6 million pounds in 1960 and then starts to rise again.

The total salmon and steelhead catch (Figure 7) was reconstructed from the amount of canned, mild-cured, and frozen salmon sold for the 1880-

[33] Forty-second Oregon Legislative Assembly, 1943, *Report of Interim Fisheries Committee* (Salem, 1945), pp. 8 and 4.

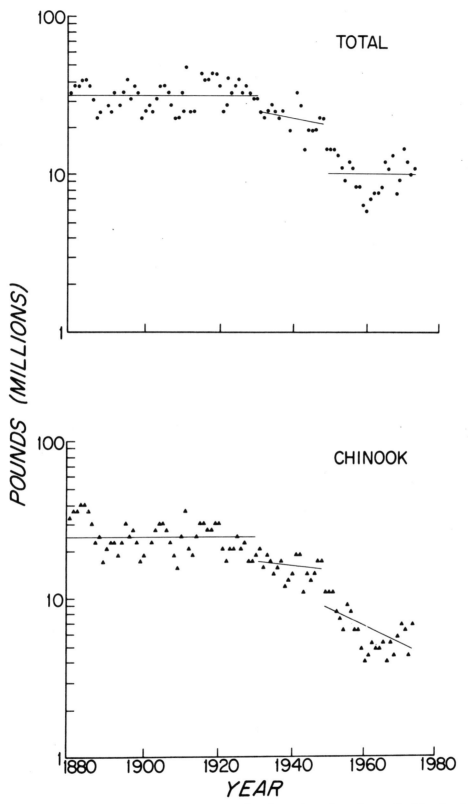

Figure 7.   Total pounds of salmon and steelhead caught and total pounds chinook salmon caught on Columbia River (1880-1930, 1931-1948, 1949-1973).

1934 period. This estimate fails to include the amount caught by Columbia Basin inhabitants—whites and Indians—for their household needs or the amount sold fresh to local markets. Based on this estimation, 1883 and 1884 appeared to be the peak years of salmon catch. Catches for these two years were estimated at 42.8 and 42.2 million pounds. Based on the same estimation procedures, however, the 1895, 1911, 1915, 1916, 1918, and 1919 catches all exceeded the 1883-1884 catches. The catch in 1925 equaled that of 1884. The time around World War I, then, was the era of peak production (Appendix B). The late teens differed from the 1880s in that all runs were fished, while in the 1880s only spring and summer chinook along with a few blueback were caught.

From 1935 to 1973, the curve in Figure 7 is constructed from salmon and steelhead landings made by inshore commercial fishers and offshore commercial trollers who landed at Columbia River ports. These data fail to include the catches by trollers and recreation anglers who catch Columbia River salmon as they migrate along the Pacific Coast from California to Alaska. The impacts of both trollers and recreation anglers were most significant after World War II.

Given the fact that the curve (Figure 7) is an approximation for the amount caught, it is possible to estimate a potential level of catch for Columbia River salmon. This would be an annual average of 33.9 million pounds salmon and steelhead landed from 1880 to 1930. This 50-year period shows no significant trend in growth or decline.

Chinook were the dominant species landed in the early years of the Columbia River salmon industry, so the lower curve in Figure 7 shows only the trends for chinook catches over the time intervals. Data were not kept by species before 1889, and all salmon caught were assumed to be chinook. With this assumption, the 1880-1930 chinook catch averages 26.4 million pounds annually, a decline of 194,000 pounds per year. For the 1931-1948 period, the average chinook catch was 16.7 million pounds and the annual rate of decline was 144,000 pounds. Finally, from 1948 to 1973, the chinook catch averaged 6.8 million pounds, declining at a rate of 209,000 pounds per year.

Chapter 9/

Beyond the Rules

COMPARING THE first quarter of the twentieth century with the 25 years following World War II (1945-1970), the Columbia River canned salmon industry declined from the third largest industry in Oregon and Washington to an industry whose output was one-third that of mining, one twenty-fifth that of agriculture, and one two-hundredth that of manufacturing. The canned salmon pack in 1972-1974 was less than 50,000 cases, a number which was surpassed in 1869, the fourth year salmon was packed on the Columbia River.

What is the explanation for this decline? Where have all the salmon gone? Were there no management programs to conserve the resource? Legislation regulating the salmon fishery specified method, time, and gear restrictions. Washington Territory created management regulations even before the canned salmon industry was started.[1] Like many "conservation" regulations, a rule passed in 1859 was more one of allocation than conservation. It prohibited nonresidents from taking fish on the beach just inside the Columbia River bar. This was one of the best beach seining grounds.

The next regulation, passed in 1866, appeared more conservation oriented. This law prohibited building a fish trap more than two-thirds the way across the Walla Walla River. But this, too, was a regulation directed at allocation, having the purpose of restricting the fishing of Indians. In Oregon, attempts at resource management began in 1878 when minimum mesh sizes and spacing between slats on traps were specified.

✦　✦　✦　✦

The primary management tool was closing certain periods to fishing. Washington instituted a closed season in 1877, and in 1878 Oregon followed suit. The closed seasons were of two types: (1) A weekly period, usually one or two days on weekends; and (2) all or parts of March, April, August, and September. In 1890 and 1891, Washington and Oregon changed the closed seasons to March 1 through April 10 and August 10 through September 10.

The enforcement of these closed seasons, however, was made a "farce of." After a 1903 inspection trip, the Oregon Master Fish Warden wrote, "I found that fishing was being carried on in all directions and no pretense whatever being made to respect the law."[2] When fishermen were caught violating the closed season, local courts failed to impose very strict penalties. Twelve trapmen were caught fishing during the closed season in 1903. Only two were found guilty, and their fine was $8

---

[1] Henry O. Wendler, "Regulation of Commercial Fishing Gear and Seasons on the Columbia River from 1859 to 1963," *Fisheries Research Papers of the Washington Department of Fisheries* 2, No. 4 (1966), p. 24.

[2] H. G. van Dusen, *Report of the Department of Fisheries of Oregon to the Legislature* (Salem, 1903), p. 7.

and court costs.[3] In 1904, there was "not a single arrest for illegal fishing during the closed season . . . 200 tierces of mild-cured salmon were put up."[4] Each tierce weighed 800 pounds and required 1,600 pounds, round weight, of salmon.[5] During World War I, canners requested suspension of the closed season. Secretary of the Interior, William Redfield, responded that the department had no intention of "acquiescing in any movement looking for the removal of the comparatively small protection now enjoyed by the salmon." Redfield also commented on the wasteful practices of cannerymen at the beginning of each season when the canneries were plugged with salmon. He said that the salmon left to rot on the beaches showed "a deplorable disregard for the future of the salmon industry and painful lack of business acumen on the part of both fishermen and packers."[6] In 1917 salmon trollers provided one company with $52,000 worth of salmon during the August 25 to September 10 closed season.[7]

Concern for the well-being of fishers, too, caused enforcement problems. The annual report of the Oregon State Board of Fish Commissioners for 1888 noted that "had the literal law been enforced this year, private property to the amount of $200,000 would have been rendered worthless, and while owing to the wealth of the packers they could have bourne the loss without serious hardship, but it is not so with the fishermen who have their all in their fishing gear."[8]

Canners supposedly supported the closed season laws. In 1882 a number of canners "subscribed a fund of $1000 to pay the Astoria chief of police to keep a close lookout for fishermen who violated the Saturday night law, but the service was not well done."[9] Fred Barker wrote Governor Withycombe in 1917 that the present laws were vital to the continuance of the industry—"to suspend the Sunday closed period would be like killing the goose that lays the golden egg."[10] Yet Barker also confided in Hammond, "Under the law, we are not supposed to fish the Willamette Slough, but a number of our St. Helens fishermen always do well there the first few days of the season, and we managed to get their fish."[11] The cannerymen needed fish to make their pack, so they bought salmon that were caught illegally. As long as a market existed, fishermen continued to find ways to catch fish.

The market for cold storage salmon created a nearly continuous demand for salmon. Cold storage salmon were mild-cured in a two-thirds salt and one-third sugar solution and sent to northern Europe for smoking and sale. Only the largest chinook salmon (weighing more than 25 pounds) and those of best quality were used. Higher prices were paid for these large salmon, usually 1 to 2 cents more per pound. The cold storage business became commercially important on the Columbia River in 1897. From 1902 to 1916 an average of 6.6 million pounds of salmon were mild-cured. Chinook salmon were sought for mild-curing; more than 25 percent of the chinook catch for these years was used for this purpose.[12] Most of the canneries had cold storage operations along with their canning operations. World War I cut off the European markets, and the cold storage trade never returned to pre-war levels.

* * * *

The cold storage market created a demand for salmon during the closed season as well as during the regular salmon seasons. With this demand and the use of gasoline engines on fishing vessels, trolling for salmon beyond the states' management jurisdiction became a significant activity. Gasoline engines made it possible to travel safely across the Columbia River bar to outside waters.

[3] *Pacific Fisherman* 1 (September 1903), p. 6.

[4] *Pacific Fisherman* 2 (May 1904), p. 8.

[5] Willis H. Rich, "Growth and Degree of Maturity of Chinook Salmon in the Ocean," *Bulletin of the Bureau of Fisheries* 39 (1926), p. 72.

[6] William G. Redfield to F. M. Warren, July 3, 1917 (Portland, Oregon Historical Society), MSS 1699, Box 6.

[7] *Astoria Evening Budget,* May 21, 1917.

[8] First and Second *Annual Reports of the State Board of Fish Commissioners* (Salem, 1889), p. 4.

[9] *Oregonian,* January 1, 1882.

[10] Fred Barker to Governor Withycombe, May 3, 1917 (Portland, Oregon Historical Society), MSS 1699, Box 40.

[11] Fred Barker to A. B. Hammond, May 4, 1923 (Portland, Oregon Historical Society), MSS 1699, Box 6.

[12] Joseph A. Craig and Robert L. Hacker, "The History and Development of the Fisheries of the Columbia River," *Bulletin of the Bureau of Fisheries* 49 (1940), p. 196.

Trolling for salmon was started near Monterey, California, in 1893 by recreation anglers. "It was carried on from sail and row boats with stout lines and hooks attached to fly rods or simply fished by hand. Sardines were used for bait."[13] Troll lines were pulled by hand. On the Columbia River, Native Americans, settlers, and recreation anglers knew that chinook and coho salmon would bite on bait or a lure. Commercial trolling in the river and off the Columbia River bar during the closed season began in the early 1900s. Many of the trollers were gillnetters who trolled to keep their boats active. A 1919 Oregon legislative report noted that trolling had "attained such momentum in the past two years that gillnetters have abandoned the gillnet except during the part of the fishing season when the big runs are on."[14] The trolling gear was cheaper, and fishermen had greater assurance of a profit. *The Chinook Observer* noted in 1916 that a troller "with small capital can make his way and his living outside, free from blistering elements and tax-eating enactments of our refined but predatory civilization."[15]

Fishery managers regarded trolling as detrimental to the salmon resource for several reasons:

1. Trollers caught immature salmon. In fact, the Association of Salmon Packers of the Columbia River placed a limit on trollers in 1920, saying they would not take salmon weighing less than 8 pounds.[16]

2. Many hooked salmon escaped from trollers. Being injured by the hook, the salmon died at sea and were lost to the fishery.

3. Troll-caught salmon were inadequate for canning. Freshwater salmon were said to be harder and less pulpy than those in saltwater. "Salmon taken in salt water does not stand up well in the can when packed," wrote Carl D. Shoemaker, "while that packed from fish taken in fresh water

remains firm."[17] These conclusions were backed up by chemical analyses which also showed that "the canning of immature fish is decidedly inferior to the standard grades in fat and protein content."[18]

When the Oregon Legislature eliminated purse seines in 1919, it also passed legislation to eliminate trolling as of January 1, 1923. The law was repealed because of lack of consensus with the state of Washington. Since the two states had entered into the Columbia River Compact in 1918, they both had to agree on management regulations. The goal set by the compact was "regulation, preservation and protection of fish in the waters of the Columbia River."[19] The principal factor in repeal of the ban on trolling was the number of trollers—1,000 to 2,000 were estimated to be fishing in 1919. Few had licenses, claiming that they fished beyond the management jurisdiction of the states.

To gain control over fishers' activities, fishery managers found it necessary to exercise control at the point of the sale. Only when they began to regulate landings did they gain control over the violations which took place beyond the limits of their management. To be effective, however, both Oregon and Washington had to adopt comparable rules so that fishermen could not play the rules of one state against the other.

Ocean trolling was an innovation fishermen used to get around the limits placed on fishing by the closed seasons. Closed seasons were considered to be the major conservation tool, but many were skeptical of their effectiveness. Pioneer canner R. D. Hume felt, "A closed-time at the beginning or end of the salmon fishing season is of no practical use, as each run of salmon comes when due almost to a day." He said, "A weekly closed-time, strictly observed, is the only method that will maintain the supply of spawning fish."[20] Yet a 1942 study by the U.S. Bureau of Fisheries showed that the salmon's average travel time from the mouth

[13] Hugh M. Smith, "Notes on a Reconnaissance of the Fisheries of the Pacific Coast of the United States in 1894," *Bulletin of the Fish Commission* 14 (1895), p. 233.

[14] Fred Barker papers, circa July 1920 (Portland, Oregon Historical Society), MSS 1699, Box 6.

[15] *The Chinook Observer*, August 11, 1916, located in Seufert Scrapbook (Portland, Oregon Historical Society), MSS 1102.

[16] *Morning Astorian*, April 30, 1920.

[17] *Telegram* article, 1922 (Portland, Oregon Historical Society), MSS 1699, Box 8.

[18] Rich, 1926, p. 16 (see note 5).

[19] "Oregon-Washington Columbia River Fish Compact," *Oregon Revised Statutes* (Portland: Daily Journal of Commerce, 1975), 507.010.

[20] R. D. Hume, "Solution of the Salmon Propagation Problem," *Pacific Fisherman* 6 (January 1908), p. 26.

Astoria trollers, 1939 (*Oregonian* photo, Oregon Historical Society).

of the Columbia to 200 miles upstream, allowing time to clear all the commercial gear, was two to three weeks.[21] With commercial gillnetters, trapmen, seiners, fishwheelers, and dipnetters all along the river, a closed period of one day per week seemed to be of little value.

Offshore trolling meant that salmon could be caught before they entered the river. Until the early 1930s, trolling took place near the mouth of the Columbia River. With the increased catch of albacore after 1936, boats that could make longer trips were capable of operating in both the albacore and salmon fisheries. Since the principal albacore season was from July through September, the salmon trolling effort increased during the months of April, May, and June. After discovering that chinook and coho could be taken in greater numbers on their feeding grounds, trollers reached outward beyond the mouth of the river.

There were more than 300 Columbia River trollers in the late 1920s; in 1933, the number had declined by half. After World War II, trolling took on new dimensions. As trollers increased in number and reached out farther, trolling became important from Monterey to southeastern Alaska. Since Columbia River chinook tend to turn north after leaving the river, many were caught by British Columbia and Alaska trollers.

✳ ✳ ✳ ✳

Tagging studies, initially made in the 1920s with limited success, documented the landings of Columbia River chinook off the coast of British Columbia and Alaska.[22] Since the late 1940s, additional tagging studies have made it possible to estimate the catch percentage in each area attributable to Columbia River-spawned salmon. Of the chinook salmon caught in southeastern Alaska and on the west coast of Vancouver Island, 45 percent

were estimated to have originated from the Columbia River. More than half of the chinook salmon caught by Washington trollers came from the Columbia River.[23]

By applying these percentages to the total chinook salmon catch in each of these areas, it is possible to estimate the quantity of chinook originating from the Columbia River. The average troll catches of Columbia River chinook in southeastern Alaska, British Columbia, Washington, and Oregon for 1969-1973 are shown in Table 16. Because of the increase in trolling, it is misleading to compare pre-World War II catch levels for salmon caught in the Columbia River with postwar levels.

Table 16. Columbia River Chinook Salmon Caught, by Area, 1969-1973

Area	Ratio, Columbia River chinook salmon attributable to area	Catch attributable to Columbia River (pounds × 10⁶)	Calculated weight loss (pounds × 10⁶)
Troll			
Southeast Alaska	.45	1.77	0.72
British Columbia, Queen Charlotte Is.	.25	0.40	0.10
British Columbia, West Coast Vancouver Is.	.45	3.19	1.66
Washington, Puget Sound	.50	0.28	0.14
Washington, Coastal	.65	1.33	0.75
Oregon, Coastal	.47	0.86	0.61
Oregon, Columbia River	.80	0.32	0.24
TOTAL		8.15	4.22
Gillnet			
Columbia River	1.00	5.17	-------

SOURCE: Thomas A. Hatley, "Efficiency in Oregon's Commercial Salmon Fisheries: A Historical Perspective" Oregon State University Master's thesis, 1976, pp. 69-86.

[21] Willis H. Rich, "The Salmon Runs of the Columbia River in 1938," *Fishery Bulletin of the Fish and Wildlife Service* 50 (1942), p. 124.

[22] Willis H. Rich and Harlan B. Holmes, "Experiments in Marking Young Chinook Salmon on the Columbia River 1916 to 1927," *Bulletin of the Bureau of Fisheries* 44 (1929), pp. 215-264; Charles H. Williamson, "Pacific Salmon Migration," *Contributions to Canadian Biology and Fisheries* 3 and 4 (1927 and 1929), pp. 267-306 and 453-470; and Alaska Territorial Fish Commission, *Research Report No. 1* (Juneau, 1921).

[23] Ed Chaney and L. Edward Perry, *Columbia Basin Salmon and Steelhead Analysis* (Portland, Pacific Northwest Regional Commission, 1976), pp. 58-59; and Thomas A. Hatley, "Efficiency in Oregon's Commercial Salmon Fisheries: A Historical Perspective," Master of Arts in Interdisciplinary Studies thesis, Oregon State University, 1976, p. 81.

For example, critics of Columbia River dams argue that in 1883 when only spring and summer chinook were caught, 42.8 million pounds of salmon were landed. Netboy stated in 1975, "In recent years, by contrast, catches have rarely exceeded 10,000,000 pounds."[24] Adjusted data, following Netboy's reasoning and considering only chinook salmon catches by Columbia River gillnetters, show a decline from the 1880-1930 catch level of 26.4 million pounds to 5.2 million pounds for 1969-1973 (Figure 8). The 1969-1973 catch does not reflect the impact of trollers, so the 8.1 million pounds caught by trollers (calculated from Table 16) should be added.

One of the early criticisms of trolling was the weight loss caused by the catch of immature salmon. A 1926 U.S. Bureau of Fisheries study indicated that trollers off the mouth of the Columbia River were catching chinook salmon a year younger than those caught in the river.[25] Subtracting the average catch weights of troll-caught sal-

mon in each area from the average weight of salmon caught in the Columbia River, and then multiplying it by the number of Columbia River chinook estimated to have been caught in each area, gives an estimate of weight loss caused by catching immature salmon. The average weight loss for 1969-1973 was calculated to be 4.2 million pounds (Table 16). This estimate is based on averages and does not account for seasonal variations. The weight loss of salmon caught off the mouth of the Columbia River was found to be highest in the spring and lowest in August and September. During the post-World War I period, most of the trolling was done in the August-September closed season. With the advent of trolling for albacore in 1936, salmon-trolling occurred earlier in the season.

A second loss factor was the problem of "shakers." These were salmon that escaped after being hooked or were released because they were undersized. Injured from being hooked, a number of the shakers could be expected to die. Data collected by van Hyning were used to estimate that the ratio of shakers that die after release to the total catch is 7.5 percent.[26] This would be an added weight loss of 0.9 million pounds. Since this latter calculation is tenuous and subject to considerable controversy, it is not included in Figure 9. The effective troll catch for 1969-1973, with a correction for weight loss due to catching immature salmon, was 12.3 million pounds; added to the 5.2 million pound gillnet catch, this gives a total of 17.5 million pounds or 66 percent of the 1880-1930 average.[27]

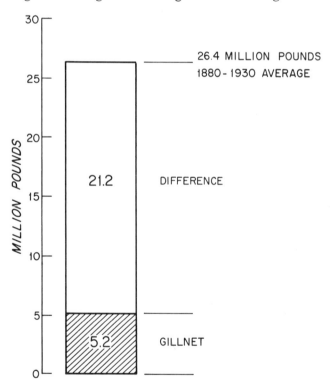

Figure 8. Pounds chinook salmon caught by gillnetters as a ratio of the 1880-1930 average chinook salmon catch.

[24] Anthony Netboy, "Where Have the Salmon Gone?" *Oregon Times* (July/August 1975), p. 12.

[25] Rich, 1926 (see note 5).

[26] Jack M. van Hyning, "Factors Affecting the Abundance of Fall Chinook Salmon in the Columbia River," Ph.D. thesis, Department of Fisheries and Wildlife, Oregon State University, 1968, pp. 185-186.

[27] In evaluating these calculations other factors should be considered. These include seasonal variations, long-term trends, the representativeness of the time periods selected, ocean mortality, interspecies relations, intermixing of runs, changed ocean and stream environments, and a variety of other factors that increase the complexity of the estimate. Because of omission of the weight loss due to shakers and the omission of the California catch of Columbia River salmon, the quantity of troll-caught Columbia River chinook is underestimated. Other factors which would also contribute to underestimation are unreported and underreported catches which would be expected because of the poundage tax collected on landings.

Catches of trollers were restricted to increase Columbia River salmon escapements (Oregon Department of Transportation).

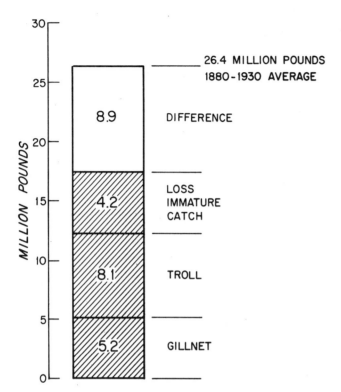

Figure 9. **Pounds chinook salmon caught by gillnetters and trollers as a ratio of the 1880-1930 average chinook salmon catch.**

These data indicate that gillnetters and trollers continued to reach into the ocean to catch salmon. The salmon caught in the ocean had not reached maximum growth. Offshore fishing also occurred in another sense not calculated here—the catches by foreign fleets. In 1965, Soviet fleets appeared off the Oregon and Washington coasts. U.S. salmon trollers provided numerous forms of evidence to demonstrate that the foreign fleets were taking what the trollers believed to be their salmon. They reported net-marked fish, seeing salmon in nets and on decks of foreign vessels, foreign vessels appearing in the midst of a good bite, disappearance of the bite after passage of foreign vessels during the night, and following the paths of foreign vessels in order to find the salmon bite.

Irrespective of whether or not these allegations were true, offshore fishers were "beyond the rules." Their existence made it difficult for fishery managers to control the impacts trollers had on management programs. Since the Columbia River Compact only provided inshore controls over domestic fishers, fishery managers had to reduce the gillnet catch to meet escapement goals. In 1938, there were 1,191 gillnetters who could fish 272 days; in 1973, there were 1,104 gillnetters and 73 fishing days.[28] The area controlled by fishery managers was limited relative to the area over which fishers roamed in search of salmon.

The United States Fisheries Conservation and Management Act of 1976 extended national jurisdiction to 200 miles and, more importantly for management of the salmon fisheries, established regional fishery management councils. The Pacific Fishery Management Council developed a plan in 1977 that restricted the catches of ocean trollers in order to increase escapements and the catches of "inside" fishers. As might be expected, this plan met with strong opposition from trollers.

Trolling is a fishing technology suitable to catching salmon before they reach the gear of inside fishers. Columbia River trolling developed initially as a way for gillnetters and other fishers to avoid the closed seasons. Following World War II, trollers seeking to intercept returning salmon were not only Columbia River fishers but also Californians, Oregonians, Washingtonians, Alaskans, Canadians, and others having favorable positions relative to management rules. The Pacific Fishery Management Council's coordinated regional plan covered Washington, Oregon, and California commercial fishers. It was a step toward broader control of fishing activity. The Council's plan to redistribute catch from trollers to inside net, recreational, and Indian fishers, was not accepted, however, without a fight.

[28] Fish Commission of Oregon and Washington Department of Fisheries, *Status Report, Columbia River Fish Runs and Commercial Fisheries, 1938-70, 1974 Addendum* (Portland, 1975), pp. 16 and 18.

Chapter 10/

Fish Fights

Do CONSERVATION RULES affect the allocation of fish resources? An affirmative answer has been given by fishermen whose gear the rules have disadvantaged. Until the mid-1970s when the counterbalancing evidence became overwhelming, fishery managers clung to the notion that "if we take the approach of maintaining the resources at maximum productivity and administering for their conservation in an impartial and scientific manner, there will be little need for concern as to who will harvest the fish."[1]

Fishers and canners who exploited the Columbia River salmon fishery were well aware that this idealism was not the case. Rather they dubbed the legal, legislative, ballot measure, and administrative conflicts over access to fisheries, "fish fights." Fish fights on the Columbia River began in the 1880s between trapmen and gillnetters, and upriver and downriver fishermen. These conflicts, as well as being fought on legal, legislative, political, and administrative grounds, at times also erupted into overt aggression.

Conflict developed between gillnetters, most of whom lived in Astoria, and trapmen fishing pound nets, most of whom lived adjacent to Baker Bay near Ilwaco on the Washington side of the Columbia. The gillnetters had organized the Columbia River Fishermen's Protective Union, which

evolved from organizations of gillnetters dating back to 1875. Gillnetters were organized for the purpose of mutual aid, proposing and opposing legislation, improving fish prices, maintaining drifts, improving safety, and preventing theft of gear. Trapmen organized into the Washington Fishermen's Association principally to counter the actions of gillnetters.

Since the best fishing areas were along the north shore of the Columbia from the mouth into Baker Bay, gillnetters and trapmen competed with one another for access to the salmon. With both groups increasing in number in the 1880s, traps were built farther out into Baker Bay into drifts which gillnetters regarded as their territory. The gillnetters charged that the trapmen's pound nets were hazardous to navigation, destructive of the resource by catching undersized fish, and the monopoly of a few.[2] The trapmen countered by claiming that the "gillnet men of Oregon" by "mob rule and riot" were greedily coveting the salmon resource by trying to intimidate the trapmen with threats of violence and wastefully throwing away fish that exceeded the capacity of canneries.[3]

Threats of violence were backed up by action. Each time a drowned gillnetter was found in or

---

[1] Fish Commission of Oregon, *Biennial Report* (1948), p. 4.

[2] Columbia River Fishermen's Protective Union, Pamphlet, 1890, pp. 4-6.

[3] Washington Fishermen's Association, *Washington Salmon Fisheries on the Columbia River* (Ilwaco, 1893), p. 2.

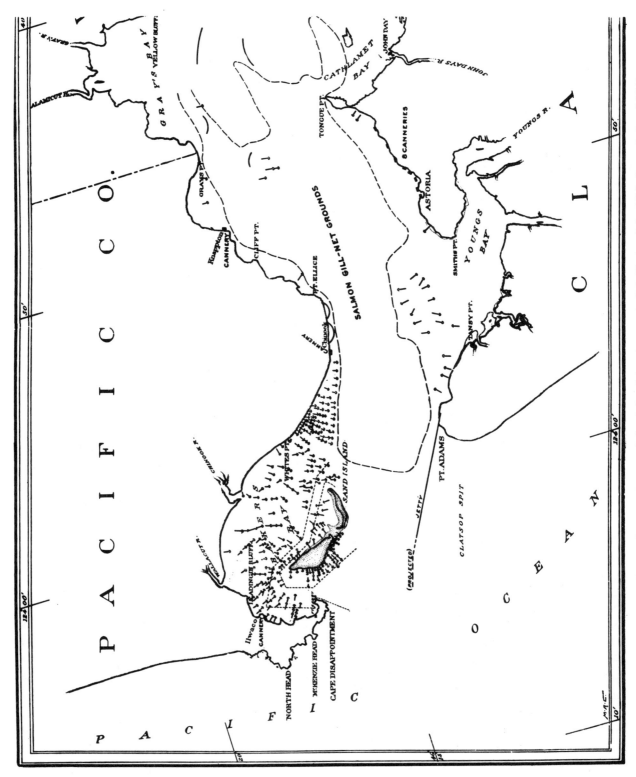

Fish traps in Baker Bay, 1892 ("The Salmon Fisheries of the Columbia River Basin," *Bulletin of the Fish Commission*, 1894).

near a pound net, the aggravation over pound nets was heightened. The gillnetter's scow, used to clear drifts, was also used on occasion to clear away pound nets thought to be illegally placed and hazardous to navigation. "With the exception of the frequent cutting of pound nets in the night no direct conflict was had with our Washington fishermen until the year 1886 at which time the union set the price to be $1 each."[4] That year the trapmen's fish were thrown overboard. In May, the next year, the *Weekly Astorian* reported, "From Ilwaco came reports of destruction of property . . . The men who destroyed the traps were masked . . . It is said that the men who did this are residents of Astoria." One man was reported killed, one wounded, and $40,000 damage was done. "It is directly asserted that the men who did Monday night's work are fishermen who view with jealousy the encroachments of traps."[5]

In the early fall of 1887 a contingent of gillnetters, attempting to organize gillnetters of Grays Harbor, Washington, north of Baker Bay, skirmished with a group of trapmen. Nine gillnetters were arrested and one later died from wounds received during the fight.[6] June 21, 1890, three members of the Columbia River Fishermen's Protective Union were killed in an attempt to prevent upriver fishermen near Rainier from fishing during a union-declared strike for higher prices.[7] During the great strike of 1896 the governors of Oregon and Washington called out their National Guards to police the actions of trapmen and gillnetters.

Violent acts such as these were but one of the tactics used in the fights between groups of fishermen. Most times fish fights were fought using legal, political, or administrative means. One example was an Oregon legislative study made in 1887, which concluded that extending the closed period from April 1 to 15, adding Saturday to the weekly Sunday closure, and building a hatchery would conserve and increase the salmon resource. On enforcement of the existing closed seasons, the committee wrote, "We think that the fine now imposed for the violation of the closed season is excessive, and for that reason it is difficult and frequently impossible to secure the conviction of persons for violation of that law."[8] To increase the enforcement capability, the committee recommended that the informer get half the recommended fine of $100 to $200. To prevent canners from furnishing gear to irresponsible fishers, the committee recommended that gear be used to pay the fine.

The legislative committee report merely heightened conflicts. Gillnetters of the Columbia River Fishermen's Protective Union noted that the chairman of the legislative committee was a recreation angler. Their pamphlet said, "We will not assert that the aforesaid gentleman never did any fishing, but we believe that such fishing as he may have done was wholly confined to angling for salmon-trout in some mountain stream, and possibly, fishing for catostomidae to vote him into office, in which latter branch of fishing he seems to have met with success."[9] These gillnetter remarks were sparked by the legislative committee's conclusion that traps, seines, and fishwheels were no more destructive of the resource than gillnets. The committee wrote that fishermen judged by "what is most advantageous to them, and argue as to the mode of fishing employed by them wholly from the standpoint of self-interest." The committee further irritated gillnetters by adding, "The trap, wheel, and like fishermen are generally riparian owners; they are resident citizens and taxpayers, while many of the gill-net fishermen are not residents of this State or Washington Territory, but come here from abroad and stay merely through the fishing season, many of them being aliens."[10]

One tool for fish fights was created by a 1902 Oregon constitutional amendment providing for initiatives and referendums. These were means by which the people of the state could both make and

---

[4] Washington Fishermen's Association, 1893, p. 3 (see note 3).

[5] *Weekly Astorian*, May 28, 1887.

[6] Columbia River Fishermen's Protective Union, Minutes (Portland, Oregon Historical Society), MSS 70 (microfilm).

[7] Columbia River Fishermen's Protective Union, June 21, 1890 (see note 6).

[8] Fourteenth Oregon Legislative Assembly, 1887, *Report of Special Committee to Examine into and Investigate the Fishing Industry of this State* (Salem, Frank C. Baker, 1893), p. 13.

[9] Columbia River Fishermen's Protective Union, 1890, p. 20 (see note 2).

[10] Fourteenth Oregon Legislative Assembly, 1893, p. 10 (see note 8).

veto laws by sponsoring ballot measure elections. One of the most interesting attempts to use the ballot box to allocate fish resources was on June 1, 1908. Two initiative petitions relating to the Columbia River salmon fishery were on the ballot. At issue were the fishing advantages of gillnetters on the lower Columbia and the fishwheel operators of the upper river. The initiative petition of the downriver fishermen, which passed, closed the upper Columbia to all gear except hook and line. This, in effect, eliminated the use of seines and fishwheels on the upper river. The initiative petition of the upriver interests, which also passed, restricted commercial fishing to daylight hours. Since night was the principal time for gillnetting, this effectively closed the lower Columbia to gillnetters.

Oregon's Master Fish Warden, H. C. McAllister, vigorously attempted to enforce these laws adopted by the people of Oregon. He arrested fishermen from both Oregon and Washington. A restraining order issued September 1908 by Circuit Court Judge William B. Gilbert prevented McAllister from enforcing the new law within the territorial limits of the state of Washington. So as not to give an unfair advantage to Washington fishermen, the injunction was then extended to include the territorial waters of Oregon, as well.[11]

The 1909 session of the Oregon Legislature, working in conjunction with the Washington Legislature, attempted to straighten out the problem but only succeeded in adding confusion by neglecting to add the words "and its tributaries" to fishery legislation jointly agreed upon by the two states. This omission left those fishing the Willamette and Clackamas rivers with an additional 15 days of fishing in March and April, while all other commercial fishermen were restricted from fishing the main stem of the Columbia and its tributaries in Washington. This omission provided a considerable advantage for the Oregon City fishermen in the spring of 1909.[12]

In 1916 the Clackamas County Fishermen's Union and Oregon City recreation anglers tried to introduce an initiative petition excluding all gear except hook and line, and gillnets. Dr. Thomas W. Ross, one of the initiative sponsors, wrote Stanford University Professor Charles H. Gilbert, "If you would write me a letter about the destructive methods of fishing, I can get the *Oregon Journal* here to help in the fight." Ross continued, "I am especially told that if I could get a statement from you concerning fishwheels, they would do the limit for the bill."[13] Gilbert's reply was, "Each form of gear is destructive just in proportion to the number of fish it catches!"[14]

By 1918 the Clackamas County Fishermen's Union was facing an initiative petition to close the Willamette River to commercial fishing. The passage of this ballot measure, sponsored by recreation anglers, ended commercial fishing in this area.

The upriver-downriver conflicts between fishers continued. Francis Seufert, whose fishery was at The Dalles, wrote that the "first year I had to go to Salem to try and protect our fishing interest was in 1887 when the union at Astoria first came into existence, and we have had union oppositions ever since."[15] An initiative petition attempted in 1922 was declared invalid by the Marion County Circuit Court. Carl D. Shoemaker claimed that the initiative petition was an attempt to "hold up" the salmon canners, and evidence was produced showing that ballot measure sponsors were associated with a request for $10,000 to expose fraudulent information about the initiative petition.[16] Referring to activities to prohibit fishwheels, traps, and seines, Barker wrote Hammond in 1922, "Past experience has shown that whenever there is a fight

[11] H. C. McAllister, *Annual Report of the Department of Fisheries of Oregon to the Legislative Assembly, Twenty-fifth Regular Session* (Salem, 1908).

[12] H. C. McAllister and R. E. Clanton, *Biennial Report of the Department of Fisheries of the State of Oregon to the Twenty-sixth Legislative Assembly, Regular Session* (Salem, 1911), p. 13.

[13] Dr. Thomas W. Ross, president of the Salmon Protective League of Oregon and Washington, to Professor Charles H. Gilbert, Stanford University, December 21, 1922 (Portland, Oregon Historical Society), MSS 1699, Box 6.

[14] Gilbert to Ross, December 30, 1922, MSS 1699, Box 6.

[15] F. A. Seufert to Albert S. Roberts, February 5, 1927 (Portland, Oregon Historical Society), MSS 1102, Box 2.

[16] *Oregonian*, August 31, 1922 (Portland, Oregon Historical Society), MSS 1699, Scrapbook, p. 54; and *Oregon Voter* 25 (November 7, 1922), p. 12.

between the upper river and lower river, the propagation and protection of the fish is always lost sight of."[17]

In 1926 gillnetters, with support from the Oregon State Grange, Oregon Federation of Labor, and Oregon Fish Commission, placed an initiative on the ballot to eliminate upriver fishwheels, traps, and seines. Opposed to the measure were the upriver processing interests who owned most of the fishwheels, primarily the Warren and Seufert families, their employees, and upriver businessmen. All the canners in Astoria, with the exception of the Union Fishermen's Cooperative, opposed the initiative. Most of the seines were owned and operated by canners who owned or leased valuable seining grounds in the lower river. Recreation anglers sided with the proponents of the initiative petition.

The accusations on each side illustrate how social and economic issues became infused with conservation arguments. Each side accused the other of monopolistic practices, absurd and untruthful assertions, and of being a threat to conservation. The initiative sponsors claimed that fishwheels were "a practical monopoly of the fishing industry on the Upper Columbia River" where "a few wealthy and powerful individuals have succeeded through enactment of special privilege laws, in virtually appropriating the right of public fishing to themselves."[18] The upriver interests countered, "The grossly unjust and un-American purpose of this dangerous bill is to monopolize the fish industry and to control—so as to raise—the price of fish to the consuming public."[19] The initiative sponsors considered the claim that only about 5 percent of the fish were caught in wheels absurd because "the fact remains that they take practically all the fish that, having escaped the gear in 150 miles of tidewater, should be entitled to proceed, to the spawning grounds to lay their eggs and perpetuate the industry."[20]

Upriver interests claimed that Columbia River salmon runs were on the increase and that claims of salmon scarcity were "designed to deceive" the voters. On this conservation issue the upriver interests followed the argument of United States Fish Commissioner Henry O'Malley, who said, "Each form of gear used is responsible for depletion in proportion to the number of fish it takes." The upriver interests went on to assert that "the greatest destroyer of salmon have been the upper-country power dams and canals."[21] The initiative sponsors countered by claiming that fishwheels took too many early spring chinook and criticized the seiners for taking too many silversides and steelhead, saying "Three seines which operate above the Cascade Rapids in pools, where tired fish stop to rest after their struggle through the turbulent waters, take hundreds of tons of fish."[22]

After the initiative passed, canners and upriver interests resorted to the courts and the legislature to reverse the decision of the people, arguing that "the initiative manner of making laws deprives those living in sparsely settled districts of proper representation, is it not un-American . . ., is it not the intention of the Constitution to afford protection to the minority?"[23] A repeal bill introduced in the 1927 Oregon Legislature failed to win support. The fact that "the general public cannot possibly have clear understanding of all these factors that enter into a proper solution of the salmon problem"[24] lost out to the argument that in repealing the "sovereign will of the people of this state" the legislator is "making himself the supreme judge instead of the people of Oregon."[25] The Oregon Legislature did reverse the "sovereign people" in 1935 and allowed the continued fishing of traps and seines.

Animosity between gillnetters and seiners continued in a 1930 fish war. "A fleet of about 25 or 30 boats, mostly from Ilwaco, Washington, drifted

---

[17]Fred Barker to A. B. Hammond, October 2, 1922 (Portland, Oregon Historical Society), MSS 1699, Box 6.
[18] Oregon Secretary of State, *Official Voters' Pamphlet, General Election, November 2, 1926* (Salem, 1926), p. 74.
[19] *Voters' Pamphlet*, 1926, p. 76 (see note 18).
[20] *Voters' Pamphlet*, 1926, p. 75 (see note 18).

[21] *Voters' Pamphlet*, 1926, p. 77 (see note 18).
[22] *Voters' Pamphlet*, 1926, p. 75 (see note 18).
[23] F. A. Seufert papers (Portland, Oregon Historical Society), MSS 1102, Box 2.
[24] *Oregon Voter* 47 (October 2, 1926), p. 4.
[25] Statement of Senator Roberts in debate on HB 354, February 14, 1927 (Portland, Oregon Historical Society), MSS 1102, Box 2.

across the seining grounds throughout the seining tides, preventing the seiners from putting out their seines."[26]

The citizens of Washington were next to make gear changes. Initiative 77, passed in 1934, eliminated all fixed gear, fishwheels, traps, seines, and set nets. It was the most sweeping gear restriction to ever affect the Columbia River. The initiative was directed more at the allocation of fisheries on Puget Sound, and its effects on the Columbia River were more incidental. On Puget Sound, purse seiners, trapmen, and gillnetters each took about one-third of the catch. The conflict there went back to the 1890s. The Washington House in 1897 voted to abolish fish traps, but the measure was killed in the Senate. Washington Initiative 51, in 1924, tried to abolish all methods except gillnets or hook and line. The initiative failed. Since traps on Puget Sound were owned by the canning companies, the conflict was more in the form of laborer versus capitalist. This type of dispute gained momentum during the depression years when high levels of unemployment led to labor arguments for reduction of the power of capitalists and a broader distribution of the fruits of productive labor. The passage of Initiative 77 eliminated 27 fishwheels, 30 drag seines, 165 set nets, and 300 trap sites on the Washington side of the Columbia.[27]

The Fish Commission of Oregon and the Washington Department of Fisheries studied the effects of Initiative 77. Their conclusion was that gillnetters and Indian dipnetters had benefited from the exclusion of fixed gear. They found no conservation benefits, saying "the gear change serves to emphasize that the elimination of one form of gear reacts to the benefit of others."[28]

The gillnetter, trapman, seiner, fishwheeler, and dipnetter proportion of the chinook salmon

catch for 1930-1934 is shown in Table 17. Gillnetter and dipnetter catch percentages increased from 1935 to 1939. Dipnetters fared best by tripling their percent of the catch. The biggest decline was in the catch of trapmen, most of whom had trap sites on the Washington side of the river. Since the Oregon Legislature had reintroduced traps and seines after they were eliminated in 1926, the Washington initiative meant a redistribution of catch to gillnetters who lived primarily in Oregon, and to Oregon trapmen and seiners.

Table 17. Impacts of Washington State Initiative 77 on Columbia River Chinook Catch

| Gear | Period | | |
	1930-1934 (%)	1935-1939 (%)	Difference (%)
Gillnet	63.8	72.3	+8.5
Trap	15.0	3.4	−11.6
Seine	16.2	14.8	−1.4
Fishwheel	1.8	0	−1.8
Dipnet	2.7	9.1	+6.4

SOURCE: D. R. Johnson, W. M. Chapman, and R. W. Schoning, "The Effects on Salmon Populations of the Partial Elimination of Fixed Fishing Gear on the Columbia River in 1935," *Oregon Fish Commission Contribution No. 11* (1948), p. 12.

The percent of chinook salmon catch for each group is shown in Table 17. Gillnetters actually caught less after the initiative than before. Only the dipnetter catch showed an increase—from 490,000 pounds in 1930-1934 to 1,365,000 pounds in 1935-1939.[29] In the 1950s their increased catch became a casualty of the dams. Construction of The Dalles Dam, beginning in 1951, inundated Celilo Falls, the major dipnetting site. When the dam was completed in 1957, the Indian catch was only 58,000 pounds. Indian fishermen developed a set net fishery as a replacement. From 1969 to 1973, the Indian set net catch averaged 1.3 million pounds.

Four groups competed for most of the Columbia River salmon—Indians, gillnetters, trollers, and recreation anglers. As has been shown, the 1880-1930 estimated sustained yield of Columbia River

[26] Newspaper article in Seufert scrapbook, August 20, 1930 (Portland, Oregon Historical Society), MSS 1102.

[27] Oregon State Planning Board, *A Study of Commercial Fishing Operations on the Columbia River* (Portland, 1938), p. 67 and Appendix B (mimeograph).

[28] D. R. Johnson, W. M. Chapman, and R. W. Schoning, "The Effects on Salmon Populations of the Partial Elimination of Fixed Fishing Gear on the Columbia River in 1935," *Oregon Fish Commission Contribution No. 11* (1948), pp. 10 and 28-32.

[29] Johnson and others, 1948, p. 12 (see note 28).

Indian dipnetters benefited from passage of Washington State Initiative 77 (University of Washington).

chinook salmon was 26.4 million pounds. From 1969 to 1973, gillnetters caught an average of 5.2 million pounds. Trollers were estimated to have taken an equivalent of 12.3 million pounds. The average catch for Columbia River Indians for the same period was 1.3 million pounds, taken in their set net fishery above Bonneville Dam. The total catch for 1969-1973 is 18.8 million pounds, 71 percent of the 1880-1930 chinook salmon average.

What about recreation anglers? What was their take? After World War II, recreation anglers were more frequent combatants in fish fights as they exerted their influence to gain allocation of the salmon resource. Recreation angling was not new

after the war. It just increased substantially in importance with rapid postwar population growth and affluence. J. Parker Whitney, in an 1893 article in *Forest and Stream*, wrote of his sports angling experience in Monterey, "I could find no record of taking salmon with rod, excepting that of my friend, Mr. A. L. Tubbs of San Francisco, from whose information I was induced to look up the fishing." Whitney learned from observing Monterey salmon trollers. He said, "My first experience was in going out with two fishermen in their boat, and in witnessing their method."[30] Apparently Whitney was not aware of Cleveland Rockwell's

[30] J. Parker Whitney, "Salmon Fishing With Bait," *Forest and Stream* (July 29, 1893), p. 77.

Recreation anglers on the Willamette River near Oregon City, 1946 (Oregon Historical Society).

VOTE 312 YES — FISH BILL!

YOUR FISH WILL SOON BE GONE

COASTAL STEELHEAD

It's Dangerous!

Going! Going! Soon GONE!!

Help save Oregon's salmon and steelhead before it is too late!

The Oregon legislature has twice passed bills with overwhelming majorities to help save OREGON'S FISH LIFE. Once in 1941 and again in 1945. Governor Earl Snell signed the bill. Each time the referendum, with less than 15,000 names, has been invoked by a few selfish fishermen to defeat our legislature. VOTE 312 X YES and help our legislature save our fish.

Anti-gillnetter ballot measure advertisement by Save Oregon Salmon and Steelhead Committee (*Oregon Northwest Angler and Hunter*, August 1946, p. 5).

1884 angling self-portrait, "Whipping the Trask," and Rudyard Kipling's angling experience at Willamette Falls in 1889.[31] Indians knew chinook and coho salmon would bite on bait or a lure. White settlers obtained salmon to meet their subsistence needs using hook and line.

The ballot measure elections after World War II took on a recreation angler versus commercial fisher theme. In 1948, Oregon recreation anglers were successful in eliminating fixed gear from the Columbia River. In 1962 and 1964, recreation anglers attempted to eliminate the Columbia River gillnet fishery. An emotional fish fight ensued. Over 1,000 Astorians on 30 buses toured the Willamette Valley to tell the people why they should vote against the recreation-angler-sponsored initiative. The initiatives failed. Recreation anglers allocated the steelhead to their bag in 1975 with the passage of an initiative prohibiting the commercial sale of steelhead. Steelhead had been declared a game fish in Washington for many years, but Washington commercial fishermen landed them in Oregon. Half of Oregon's steelhead landings came from Washington fishermen. Some recreation anglers were less conservation minded, and their arguments dealt more directly with the allocation of fish. A recreation angler newsletter said, "It's a lot more sport to catch a salmon on a hook and line than to open a can."[32]

Recreation anglers fished for salmon from the upper reaches of the Columbia River and its tributaries, along the mainstream, and offshore. They fished as individuals and from ocean-going charter boats. On a charter boat trip, the recreation angler paid to be taken to the fish, reducing the time spent per fish caught. To catch a Willamette River salmon required an average time of 39 hours. In the ocean, the average time was 10 hours.[33]

Recreation angler catches (Figure 10) were estimated based on surveys, individual reports,

[31] Franz Stenzel, *Cleveland Rockwell, Scientist and Artist, 1837-1907* (Portland, Oregon Historical Society, 1972), p. 94; and Rudyard Kipling, "A Classic Fish Story," *The American Angler* 2 (December 1917), pp. 415-420.

[32] Multnomah Anglers and Hunters Club, *Newsletter* (September 1974), p. 2.

[33] *Oregon Game Commission Bulletin* 27 (1972), p. 9.

and similar data. There were no weight records, and all available data were in numbers of fish. Oregon and Washington had about one million recreation anglers in 1973. Their average catch per angler was approximately two salmon annually. The average annual chinook salmon catch for recreation anglers was estimated from data

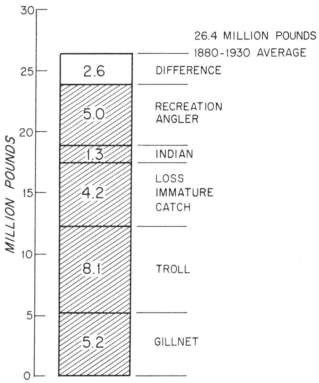

Figure 10. Pounds chinook salmon caught by gillnetters, trollers, Indians, and recreation anglers as a ratio of the 1880-1930 average chinook salmon catch.

compiled by the Pacific Marine Fisheries Commission. These data were corrected for the estimated number of Columbia River chinook caught by Washington, Oregon, Idaho, and California recreation anglers. No data were available for British Columbia, so the same ratio for the commercial catch was assumed and corrected for population differences. A correction for landing immature salmon was also included. The result was an estimated 5.0 million pounds of Columbia River chinook salmon caught by recreation anglers. Adding this to the 18.8 million pounds caught by gillnetters, Indians, and trollers gives a total of 23.8 million pounds—90 percent of the 1880-1930 average chinook salmon catch.

Two-thirds of the perceived loss of chinook salmon is actually explained by redistribution of catch to commercial trollers and recreation anglers (Figure 10). Nearly half, 47 percent, of the estimated 1880-1930 potential chinook catch was made by trollers in 1969-1973. Twenty-five percent was made in the river by gillnetters and Indian set net fishermen. The remainder, 10 percent, can be attributed to loss of habitat. In addition, much greater dependence was placed on fall chinook runs and hatchery-produced salmon.

Clearly, the fish fights resulted in a redistribution of catch among fishers. Initiative 77 merely changed the catch percentages among the various competing groups. No conservation benefits were noted. The number of trollers and recreation anglers increased following World War II, leading to their capture of a greater proportion of the salmon. Redistribution, more than loss of habitat, accounts for the decline in poundage landed by inside fishers. Ballot measure elections resulted in elimination of fishwheelers, trapmen, and seiners. Dipnetters were eliminated by dam construction. Trolling developed as an adaptation to closed seasons and trollers reached farther and farther outward for salmon. Population growth and affluence increased the number of recreation anglers, who competed both at the ballot box and in the fishery to include salmon in their bag.

Chapter 11/

Fish for Food

WHAT HAS BEEN the result of a century of conflict over who will benefit from the Columbia River salmon fishery? Can the issues of the fish fights be settled and the conflict ended?

Several events in 1976 raised new expectations for solving conflicts over access to Columbia River salmon. Court decisions established specific quantities which were due Native Americans. The Pacific Fishery Management Council attempted to allocate fairly the available salmon and to increase escapements so the catch could expand. History of the preceding century of the Columbia River fishery, however, suggests that as long as the desires of users exceed the quantity of salmon available, a solution is unlikely.

The Columbia River salmon fishery has changed significantly as fishers, processors, consumers, and other people associated with it have adjusted to management regulations and alternative uses of the river's resources. Still, internal conflicts remain within the fishery. A larger problem is the competition between the ever-growing number of users and variety of uses of the river. How much can the Columbia River sustain?

* * * *

F. M. Warren summarized the problem of competing uses in 1923. "Civilization," said Warren, "is the enemy of wildlife and the development of irrigation and power projects, logging and other enterprises have in many cases ruined the natural spawning grounds and seriously menaced the future of the fishing business."[1] Loss of spawning habitat to competing uses changed the timing and availability of salmon runs. In the 1880s, catches were principally of spring and summer chinook. The season peak was during mid-June. After 1900, the season's peak shifted to early August.

Since the 1930s, more and more dams have impeded upstream and downstream salmon migrations. In 1975, the spring season for commercial gillnetting was closed; the summer season had been closed since 1964. Fall was the major fishing season for inshore fishers. They depended heavily on the fall chinook and coho runs that hatcheries had successfully increased following transformation of the Columbia into a series of slack water pools. With augmentation from the hatcheries, catches in the 1969-1973 period, adjusted for catching immature salmon, were 90 percent of the 1880-1930 average.

Decline of natural runs was viewed by many as a severe loss. This cut into the enjoyment of recreation anglers, who believed that naturally spawned salmon fought harder and were better quality. To the commercial fishers, especially the inshore gillnetters who remembered great runs and great sal-

[1] F. M. Warren to W. J. Barden, U. S. Engineers Office, December 31, 1923 (Portland, Oregon Historical Society), MSS 1699, Box 6.

mon of the past or stories told by their fathers and grandfathers, the hatchery effort fell far short of their expectations.

*   *   *   *

The winter of 1976-1977 was the driest on record. This drought highlighted the fact that the Columbia River serves many uses in addition to fisheries. Hydroelectric generation, agriculture, business, transportation, and recreation competed for a share of the Columbia's resources just as the various groups of salmon fishers had done. Further, changes in one segment of the fishery to meet these non-fishery needs have effects which radiate through many parts of the fishery.

The Dalles Dam, completed in 1957, is an illustration. Construction of the dam provided people many benefits—electricity, navigation, recreation, and flood control. To achieve these benefits, the Celilo Falls Indian dipnet fishery was eliminated. The commercial salmon catch by Native Americans in 1955 was nearly two million pounds. The next year it dropped to 910,000 pounds and by 1957 their catch was only 58,000 pounds.[2] The Indians were compensated for the loss of their Celilo fishery, but how can a group of people be compensated for a renewable resource which is an intimate part of their culture?

Joining with the emerging civil rights movement of the 1960s, the Indians claimed that fishery managers were using conservation rules to discriminate against them. A group of Columbia River Indians, the "So Happy Plaintiffs," brought suit for violation of the 1855 treaty. In his 1969 decision, Judge Robert Belloni ruled "Indian treaties, like international treaties, entered into by the United States are part of the supreme law of the land." Belloni noted three limitations on the state's power to regulate the Indians' federal treaty rights to fish—"The regulation must be necessary for conservation of fish; the state restrictions on Indian treaty fishing must not discriminate against Indians; and they must meet appropriate standards."[3]

Indian fishermen were still not convinced they were being treated fairly, and additional court actions were initiated. For Puget Sound, the February 12, 1974 Boldt Decision, interpreted the 1855 treaty words "in common" to mean the opportunity for taking equal shares. Judge Boldt ruled, " 'In common with' means sharing equally the opportunity to take fish at 'usual and accustomed grounds and stations.' "[4] In rejecting the appeal of this decision, Judge Burns of appeals court noted, "It has been recalcitrance of Washington State officials (and their vocal non-Indian commercial and sports fishing allies) which produced the denial of Indian rights requiring intervention by the district court."[5] The equal shares concept was extended to the Columbia River by Judge Belloni on May 8, 1974.[6]

These court decisions were steps by Native Americans toward regaining the rights negotiated in the treaties of 1855. The treaty rights were never fully granted because of the previous actions of courts, white settlers, fishery managers, and Columbia Basin developers. The Belloni and Boldt decisions clarified the phrase, "to take fish in common with the citizens of the territory." This phrase was never clearly understood. In 1881 and 1882, U.S. Indian Commissioner Hiram Price wrote to the Secretary of the Interior noting how white landowners were attempting to exclude Indian entry to their usual and accustomed fishing places. Price said,

> I can readily understand how the framers of the treaty foresaw the importance and justice of securing an equal privilege with the Indians in this vast natural storehouse for the perhaps almost equally needy settlers. . . . and so it was, in my opinion, that the words "in common with the citizens of the territory" came to be inserted, not with a view to limiting the duration of the privilege on the supposition that the rights of "citizens of the Territory" would cease at some future period, but rather to give to the settlers there an equal privilege in that which heretofore had been exclusively enjoyed by the Indians.[7]

---

[2] Fish Commission of Oregon and Washington Department of Fisheries, *Status Report, Columbia River Fish Runs and Commercial Fisheries, 1938-70* (Portland, 1971), p. 62.

[3] 302 F. Supp. 899 (1964).

[4] 384 F. Supp. 312 (1974), at p. 343.

[5] 520 F. 2d. 676 (1975), at p. 693.

[6] Civil No. 68-409, U.S. District Court, Oregon, May 10, 1974, also August 26, 1975.

[7] Hiram Price, *Report to the Secretary of the Interior, April 14, 1882* (U.S. Office of Indian Affairs, Report Books, April 13-July 24, 1882), p. 24 (microfilm).

Celilo Falls dipnet fishery was inundated by The Dalles Dam in 1957 (*Seattle Times*).

Price's point was that " 'in common with the citizens of the Territory' was not employed to restrict or limit the rights of the Indians, but rather to afford a common privilege to the citizens of the territory."[8] "In common" then, did not in Price's mind refer to rights given Indians by the 1855 treaty, but "in common" meant that whites were taking fishing rights from the Indians because the Columbia River salmon resource "was too great a franchise to perpetuate to Indians exclusively."[9] Interestingly, Frederick Cramer, a white who became a Celilo Falls dipnetter, expressed a very similar view. "Although the Celilo Falls area was the historic fishing ground of the Indians," said Cramer, "the treaty of 1855 specified that white men could fish in common with the Indians."[10]

Implementing the court decisions to increase the Indian's salmon catch required taking salmon from those already fishing. The proposal to accomplish this was to shorten the ocean troll season for those trollers whose fishing affected Columbia River chinook salmon runs. As might be expected, trollers objected to this plan. They argued that troll-caught salmon filled an important market need. They said that troll-caught salmon were of better quality and met the timing of market demands better than those caught by inside fishers. The higher prices paid trollers imply support for their argument. Sixty years ago the lower price paid for troll-caught salmon was explained, "Salmon taken in salt water does not stand up well in the can when packed."[11] Arguments such as this one were used, at that time, in attempts to eliminate trolling!

The needs, then, of other users of the Columbia River's resources merely aggravated the problem of too many fishers. The fishery had more fishers than the resource could support. Many uses of the Columbia in electric power generation, irrigation, pollution abatement, and so on, competed with the salmon fishery. These uses were beyond the control of fishery managers, but they affected the quantity of salmon available to fishers.

* * * *

These lessons in the history of a century of Columbia fisheries show that court, regional fishery management council, and other new management concepts were just part of a long series of actions by fishers, processors, and others associated with the fishery to limit access to the salmon. Quite naturally each disadvantaged group felt that their rights in a free enterprise system were violated. Free enterprise was the issue raised most often by fishers when discussing limited entry proposals to decide who could obtain fishing licenses.

Freedom of enterprise is a relative concept. It was never applied equally to all peoples who sought to catch salmon. Certainly, Native Americans were not granted freedom of enterprise, nor was freedom of enterprise granted Chinese cannery workers who tried gillnetting. During the early twentieth century, legislation excluding aliens attempted to keep immigrant fishermen and cannery workers out of the fishery. Fish fights indicate that at one time or another various groups sought to restrict one another's fishing activities.

Free enterprise in a fishery should accomplish three goals—improve fishers' wages, maintain owners' profits, and provide consumers with a good quality, basic food item at a lower price. Only during the first 20 years of Columbia River salmon fishing were these goals of free enterprise met (Figure 11). The 1866-1884 period covers less than one-fifth of the time discussed in the history of the salmon fishery. After this "golden age," owners' profits declined, prices paid fishers stabilized, and prices to consumers increased.

World War I stimulated new production highs. The numbers of fishers, canners, and consumers increased, but they were reduced again in the depression of the 1930s. After World War II, salmon was consumed more in the context of a "fancy food article." Trollers became the principal suppliers to restaurants, specialty markets, and tourists. Higher prices excluded consumption of sal-

---

[8] Price, 1882, p. 25 (see note 7).

[9] Price, 1882, p. 25 (see note 7).

[10] Frederick K. Cramer, "Recollections of a Salmon Dipnetter," *Oregon Historical Quarterly* 75 (September 1974), pp. 230-231.

[11] Carl D. Shoemaker, "Facts Relating to Outside or Ocean Fishing," draft of article written for the *Telegram*, circa 1922 (Portland, Oregon Historical Society), MSS 1699, Box 6.

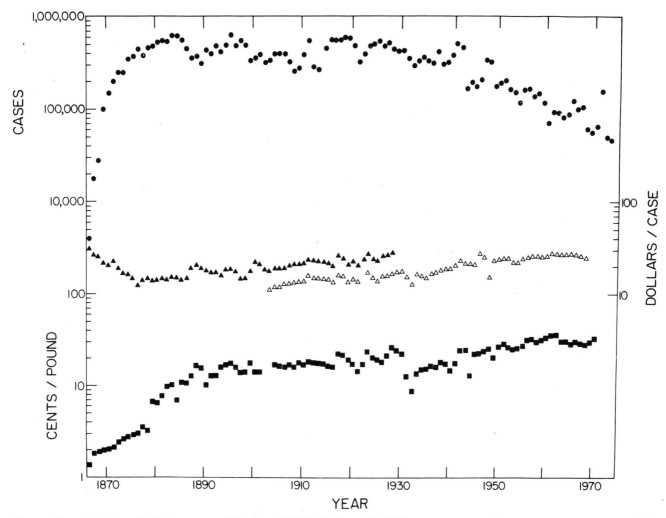

Figure 11. A brief period of commercialization, 1866-1884, benefited fishers, canners, and consumers. ● = cases packed, ▲ = opening price talls, △ = opening price halves, ■ = price received by gillnetters.

mon as a basic food item. Management regulations became more restrictive, and recreation anglers sought an increased share of the salmon catch.

As the salmon fishery lost its capacity to improve workers' wages, maintain owners' profits, and reduce consumers' costs, it began to lose its power to compete with other uses of Columbia River water resources. In spite of hatchery development, improved management techniques, and attempts to adapt on the part of fishers, processors, and others associated with the fishery, the Columbia River salmon fishery, after the 1920s, experienced a long, slow, undramatic erosion from importance. The erosion resulted from the cumulative effects of the actions of fishers, canners, consumers, resource managers, citizens, and basin

developers, each trying to solve the problems confronting the salmon industry as social priorities and uses of the Columbia River's resources changed. No one person, event, or activity can be blamed for the decline. Because the salmon resource was limited, it could only satisfy a limited number of people. The salmon industry declined as people, one by one, came to depend on other resources.

Columbia River salmon no longer met the basic food needs of industrial workers; salmon were used more to provide fish for fun. Perhaps the old gillnetter was right. Perhaps it was too late. Perhaps discussion of limited entry in the 1970s reflected more the condition of the fishery than a solution to the persistent problem of too many fishers.

A century after salmon canning rose to importance, most Columbia River salmon were caught in the ocean by trollers and sold fresh or frozen.

The condition of the Columbia River salmon fishery in the 1970s was not unique. It appeared to have evolved through a set of conditions typical of other fisheries exploited for food. Like other fisheries, the fish caught no longer met basic food needs. Social priorities changed, and there was competition over access to the resource. Rather than benefiting larger and larger numbers of people, the salmon resource was increasingly restricted.

Would the result have been different if another set of economic, social, and political conditions had surrounded the Columbia River fishery? Other case studies of fisheries development must be analyzed to answer this question. Fisheries in which many nations have participated appear to have faced similar problems. Many fisheries, including the whale; Peruvian anchovy; North Atlantic cod, haddock, swordfish, and lobster; and Pacific perch, halibut, and shrimp, have faced decline after limited periods of rapid growth and success. All have failed to strike a long-term balance in providing benefits to fishers, processors, and consumers.

Growth and decline will continue in most commercial fisheries. Possibly commercial fisheries will evolve, as did land-based hunting and gathering, from capture to culture. Agriculture provides most of the food for the majority of peoples. Quite likely the use of fish resources will follow this same evolutionary path in which capture gives way to culture. This pattern of evolution will not help the gillnetter, trapman, seiner, fishwheeler, dipnetter, troller, or any of the other fishers. They will continue to attempt to stem the flow of events by which they have been excluded from salmon allocations. Resource allocation is a persistent problem—one that always needs solution but defies being solved. The history of the Columbia River salmon fishery for more than 100 years points to a continuance of a process where increasingly select groups of fishers, processors, and consumers compete with one another for a limited resource.

Is the case of the Columbia River salmon fishery unique? Or is it an illustration of the problems that result when people's needs exceed the capacity of resources to support them?

Appendix A.   Numbers of Columbia River Gear, 1874-1937

Year	Gillnet boats	Traps	Haul seines	Fish-wheels	Dipnets	Trollers	Source
1874	250						1
1875	300						1
1876	400						1
1877	450	4	5				1,2
1878	550						1
1879	750						1
1880	900						1
1881	1,200	20					1,3
1882	1,500			1			1
1883	1,700			4			1
1884	1,500			5			4
1885		105					1
1886		154					1
1887	1,600	156		7			5
1888	1,435						1
1889	1,226	164	40	40	110		1,6
1890	1,224	168	35	41	103		1,6
1891	1,410	238	49	44	83		1,6
1892	1,536	378	38	57	75		1,6
1893							
1894	2,200						1
1895	2,207	378	84	57			1,7
1896							
1897							
1898							
1899				76			1
1900							
1901							
1902							
1903							
1904	2,596[a]	393	92	49			1,8
1905							
1906							
1907							
1908							
1909	2,348[b]	346	52	51			1,9
1910							
1911							
1912[c]							1
1913							
1914							
1915	2,856	301	59		500		10
1916							
1917							
1918							
1919					1,000		1
1920[d]							1
1921							
1922							
1923	1,604						1
1924							
1925	1,605		55	62	322	365	1,11
1926	1,790	506	94	48	291	342	1,11
1927	1,885	451	98	54	307	321	1,11
1928[e]	1,589	374	104	30	331	349	1,11
1929	1,741	412	96	34	346	461	1,11

Appendix A.   Numbers of Columbia River Gear, 1874-1937 (Continued)

Year	Gillnet boats	Traps	Haul seines	Fish-wheels	Dipnets	Trollers	Source
1930	1,608	442	98	39	306	442	1,12
1931	1,495	289	86	32	310	261	1,12
1932	1,307	207	49	29	261	183	1,12
1933	1,353	239	63	29	290	155	1,12
1934	1,359	238	57	27	311	179	1,12
1935[f]	1,225	51	44	0	477	193	12
1936	1,239	38	42	0	471	206	12
1937	1,174	27	44	0	385	194	12
1938	1,193	32	31	0	431	273	12
1939							13

[a] Only 43 were powerboats.

[b] One-sixth were powerboats.

[c] Trolling off the mouth of the Columbia was initiated.

[d] First appearance of one-man gillnet boats; before most were two-man.

[e] Fishwheels illegal in Oregon. Number of two-man gillnet boats exceed one-man.

[f] Pound nets, seines, and fishwheels illegal in Washington.

SOURCES:

1. Joseph A. Craig and Robert L. Hacker, "The History and Development of the Fisheries of the Columbia River," *Bulletin of the Bureau of Fisheries* 49 (1940).

2. *Weekly Astorian.*

3. *Oregonian,* January 1, 1882.

4. Columbia River Fishermen's Protective Union, Pamphlet (Astoria, 1890).

5. W. A. Jones, *The Salmon Fisheries of the Columbia River* (Washington, D.C., 1887), Senate Executive No. 123, First Session, Fiftieth Congress, Serial Set No. 2510.

6. William A. Wilcox, "Fisheries of the Pacific Coast," *Report of the Commissioner of Fish and Fisheries for the Year Ending June 30, 1893* (Washington, D.C., 1895).

7. William A. Wilcox, "Notes on the Fisheries of the Pacific Coast in 1895," *Report of the Commissioner of Fish and Fisheries for the Year Ending June 30, 1896* (Washington, D.C., 1898).

8. William A. Wilcox, *The Commercial Fisheries of the Pacific Coast States in 1904* (Washington, D.C., 1907), Bureau of Fisheries Document No. 612.

9. John N. Cobb, *The Salmon Fisheries of the Pacific Coast* (Washington, D.C., 1911), Bureau of Fisheries Document No. 751.

10. Lewis Radcliffe, *Fishery Industries of the United States* (Washington, D.C., 1919), Bureau of Fisheries Document No. 875.

11. See yearly issues of *Fishery Industries of the United States* (Washington, D.C., 1925-1938), Bureau of Fisheries documents.

12. *Fishery Industries of the United States* (Washington, D.C., 1932-1941), Administrative Reports of the Commissioner of Fisheries.

13. After 1938, see *Fishery Statistics of the United States* (Washington, D.C., 1942-   ), National Marine Fisheries Service Statistical Digest.

Appendix B. Price and Quantity Data for Columbia River Salmon Fishery, 1866-1973

Year	No. of Columbia River canneries	All species		Chinook salmon						Consumer Price Index (1957-1959 100)
		Pounds caught	Cases packed	No. of cases	Value ($)	Opening price ($)		Price paid gillnetters (cents per lb.)		
						Halves	Talls	Average	Official	
1866	1	272,000	4,000				16.00	0.7	0.8	51.0
1867	1	1,224,000	18,000				13.00	0.9	1.0	49.0
1868	2	1,904,000	28,000				12.00	0.9	1.0	47.0
1869	4	6,800,000	100,000				10.00	0.9	1.0	46.0
1870	5	10,200,000	150,000				9.00	0.9	1.0	44.0
1871	6	13,600,000	200,000				9.50	0.9	1.0	42.0
1872	6	17,000,000	250,000				8.00	01.0	1.1	42.0
1873	8	17,000,000	250,000				7.00	01.0	1.2	42.0
1874	13	23,800,000	350,000				6.50	01.1	1.2	40.0
1875	14	25,500,000	375,000				5.60	01.1	1.2	38.0
1876	17	30,600,000	450,000				4.50	01.1	1.2	37.0
1877	29	25,840,000	380,000				5.20	01.3	1.2	37.0
1878	30	31,280,000	460,000				5.00	01.1	1.2	34.0
1879	30	32,640,000	480,000				4.60	02.2	2.5	33.0
1880	35	36,040,000	530,000				4.80	02.2	2.5	34.0
1881	35	37,400,000	550,000				5.00	02.6	3.0	34.0
1882	35	36,808,400	541,300				4.80	03.3	3.8	34.0
1883	39	42,799,200	629,400				5.00	03.3	3.8	33.0
1884	37	42,160,000	620,000				4.75	02.2	2.5	32.0
1885	37	37,658,400	553,800				4.50	03.4	3.8	32.0
1886	39	30,498,000	448,500				4.75	03.3	3.8	32.0
1887	39	24,208,000	356,000				6.00	04.0	4.5	32.0
1888	28	25,328,436	372,477				6.50	05.2	5.0	32.0
1889	21	21,072,180	309,885	266,697	1,600,182		6.00	04.9	5.0	32.0
1890	21	29,632,632	435,744	335,604	1,946,087		5.60	03.1	5.0	32.0
1891	22	27,128,804	398,953	353,907	2,038,566		5.40	04.0		32.0
1892	24	33,138,984	487,338	344,267	1,996,388		5.40	04.0	5.0	32.0
1893	24	28,279,568	415,876	288,773	1,559,374		5.28		5.0	32.0
1894	24	33,326,800	490,100	351,106	1,896,976		5.40		5.0	30.0
1895	24	43,159,328	634,696	444,909	2,428,658		5.28	05.0	5.0	29.0
1896	24	32,755,396	481,697	370,943	1,804,511		5.00		4.5	29.0
1897	2	38,025,028	552,721	432,753	1,804,221		4.20		4.0	29.0
1898	23	33,950,192	487,933	329,566	1,490,394		4.20		4.0	29.0
1899	17	24,003,632	332,774	255,824	1,458,175		5.00	05.0	6.0	29.0
1900	16	25,798,996	358,772	262,392	1,821,258		6.40		4.0	29.0
1901	13	29,832,444	390,183				6.00		4.0	29.0
1902	14	26,200,024	317,143	270,580	1,428,743	3.40	5.40			30.0
1903	16	30,488,736	339,577	301,762	1,610,614	3.40	5.40			31.0
1904	20	36,863,872	395,104	320,378	1,944,690	3.60	5.80	05.2	5.0	31.0
1905	19	37,800,064	397,273	327,106	1,962,636	3.60	5.80		5.0	31.0

Appendix B. Price and Quantity Data for Columbia River Salmon Fishery, 1866-1973 (Continued)

Chinook salmon

Year	No. of Columbia River canneries	All species — Pounds caught	All species — Cases packed	No. of cases	Value ($)	Opening price ($) Halves	Opening price ($) Talls	Price paid gillnetters (cents per lb.) Average	Price paid gillnetters (cents per lb.) Official	Consumer Price Index (1957-1959 = 100)
1906	19	35,653,064	394,898	311,334	1,868,007	4.00	6.00		5.0	32.0
1907	19	28,720,628	324,171	258,443		4.20	6.60		5.5	33.0
1908	14	24,340,892	253,341	210,096		4.20	6.60		5.0	32.0
1909	15	24,535,328	274,087	162,131	1,203,546	4.20	6.60			32.0
1910	15	35,330,420	391,415	244,285	1,882,137	4.40	7.00	05.6	5.5	33.0
1911	15	49,480,008	543,331	405,862	2,204,185	5.20	7.80		6.0	33.0
1912	15	27,530,198	285,666	220,317	1,988,526	5.00	7.80		6.0	34.0
1913	15	26,556,172	266,479	192,116	1,664,670	5.00	7.80		6.0	34.5
1914	17	38,501,303	454,621	289,464	2,573,502	5.00	7.80		6.0	35.0
1915	19	43,838,680	558,534	406,486	3,694,361	5.00	7.60	05.8		35.4
1916	20	42,746,340	547,805	395,166	3,572,203	5.00	7.60		6.0	38.0
1917	20	40,447,986	555,218	403,637	5,023,529	7.00	11.60		10.0	44.7
1918	20	44,125,423	591,381	400,952	5,222,983	8.00	12.60		11.3	52.4
1919	21	44,934,497	580,028	392,125	5,455,550	8.00	12.60		11.3	60.3
1920	22	36,311,560	481,545	420,467	5,661,580	10.00	15.60		12.0	69.8
1921	20	26,712,547	323,241	267,582	3,761,321	8.40	12.60		9.0	62.3
1922	23	30,152,657	392,174	237,230	3,724,393	13.00	13.60		10.0	58.4
1923	23	35,667,250	480,925	289,586	4,967,657	10.00	16.00	14.0	14.0	59.4
1924	22	38,167,054	500,872	293,716	4,508,236	8.80	14.20	11.9	12.0	59.6
1925	21	42,333,443	540,452	250,809	5,423,129	8.40	14.00	11.5	12.0	61.1
1926	21	35,566,659	479,723	295,302	4,744,131	9.40	15.80	10.9	13.5	61.6
1927	22	37,688,415	519,809	339,446	5,559,202	9.40	15.80	12.9	14.0	60.5
1928	24	33,127,066	446,646	251,404	4,355,218	9.80	16.60	15.6	15.0	59.7
1929	21	32,321,281	422,117	242,938	4,234,214	10.20		14.3	17.0	59.7
1930	21	31,923,399	429,505	281,346	4,092,810	10.00		12.6	17.0	58.0
1931	20	27,031,840	353,699	294,798	3,754,929	8.00		06.6	10.0	53.0
1932	15	23,330,217	296,191	216,511	2,023,390	6.00		04.1	6.0	47.6
1933	14	26,846,800	336,711	251,157	2,719,303	7.30		06.0	8.5	45.1
1934	13	27,901,937	362,721	251,068	2,630,152	7.20		06.9	10.0	46.6
1935	10	25,756,006	332,739	205,870	2,479,450	7.10		07.2	10.0	47.8
1936	11	23,528,578	316,445	220,188	2,964,058	8.00		07.9	11.0	48.3
1937	11	26,108,200	416,830	291,343	4,256,819	8.40		07.9	13.0	50.0
1938	10	18,833,900	307,990	173,892	2,707,267	8.80		08.7	12.0	49.1
1939	10	17,910,500	322,472	207,595	3,336,206	8.90		08.2	12.0	48.4
1940	11	19,340,100	386,999	244,570	3,785,681	9.00		07.1	12.5	48.8
1941	11	31,602,700	513,712	328,609	5,558,254	10.40		08.9	13.5	51.3
1942	12	26,546,200	464,401	274,750	5,692,929	13.00		13.8	15.5	56.8
1943	11	14,753,300	167,660	130,373	3,094,505	13.00		14.4	17.0	60.3
1944	10	17,643,200	196,762	163,047	3,714,591	13.00		07.9	17.0	61.3

Appendix B. Price and Quantity Data for Columbia River Salmon Fishery, 1866-1973 (Continued)

Year	No. of Columbia River canneries	All species		Chinook salmon						Consumer Price Index (1957-1959 = 100)
		Pounds caught	Cases packed	No. of cases	Value ($)	Opening price ($)		Price paid gillnetters (cents per lb.)		
						Halves	Talls	Average	Official	
1945	8	17,368,600	175,670	132,014	3,095,228	13.00		13.7		62.7
1946	11	18,078,100	209,471	159,872	5,940,740	18.50		15.1		68.0
1947	10	21,664,000	347,306	250,318	8,613,000	19.50		18.4		77.8
1948	12	21,246,600	324,242	235,310	9,342,000	22.75		20.9		83.8
1949	12	13,050,700	178,122	133,347	3,682,000	19.00		16.7		83.0
1950	11	13,303,900	192,990	136,635	4,964,201	20.00		22.3		83.8
1951	10	12,913,200	203,125	143,046	5,497,305	22.00		26.0		90.5
1952	9	10,724,300	167,616	95,353	3,506,181	22.50		24.1		92.5
1953	8	9,720,500	153,199	97,320	3,267,303	20.50		23.0		93.2
1954	8	7,647,000	119,057	71,993	2,550,257	20.50		23.8		93.6
1955	8	10,804,200	161,557	117,782	4,392,455	22.50		25.5		93.3
1956	8	9,783,100	167,121	112,076	4,328,650	23.50		29.8		94.7
1957	8	7,323,000	138,016	87,420	3,738,912	25.00		31.3		98.0
1958	7	8,114,300	149,258	82,786	3,714,465	25.50		30.0		100.7
1959	10	6,065,100	118,246	70,149	2,942,503	25.50		32.1		101.5
1960	8	5,219,000	72,770	50,285	2,328,334	26.50		34.6		103.1
1961	8	5,433,800	94,852	57,014	3,420,840	28.70		37.0		104.2
1962	8	6,890,500	92,044	64,437	3,098,600	28.50		38.1		105.4
1963	8	5,883,500	82,374	52,213	2,399,052	29.00		32.3		106.7
1964	8	6,964,600	88,226	52,620	2,328,838	29.00		33.0		108.1
1965	8	8,583,800	127,471	72,550	3,398,776	30.00		31.5		109.9
1966	7	8,422,800	100,210	42,099	1,963,431	30.00		34.3		113.1
1967	6	9,442,000	105,476	42,768	1,986,935	30.00		33.8		116.3
1968	6	5,579,800	61,290	25,678	1,154,724	30.00		34.6		121.2
1969	5	8,038,000	57,352	29,057	1,391,758	30.00		38.6		127.7
1970	6	12,579,400	66,356	21,025	1,231,968	31.00		45.2		135.3
1971	8	9,004,100	155,956	38,247	1,648,848	35.00				141.0
1972	7	7,882,700	50,629	25,325	1,520,478					145.7
1973	8	10,821,200	47,530	22,107	1,840,095					

SOURCES: **Number of fish canneries, cases of chinook salmon packed, and value of chinook salmon packed:** Joseph A. Craig and Robert L. Hacker, "The History and Development of the Fisheries of the Columbia River," *Bulletin of the Bureau of Fisheries* 49 (1940); various issues of *Pacific Packers Report*, annual supplement to *National Fisherman*.

Pounds caught, all species: 1899 to 1936, Craig and Hacker (1940), Table 23; for 1937, *Fishery Industries of the United States* (Washington, D.C., 1940), Administrative Reports of the Commissioner of Fisheries; 1938 to 1973, Fish Commission of Oregon and Washington Department of Fisheries, *Status Report, Columbia River Fish Runs and Fisheries, 1974 Addendum* (Portland, 1975).

Cases packed, all species: Craig and Hacker (1940); various issues of *Pacific Fisherman* and *Pacific Packers Report*.

Opening price, halves and talls: John N. Cobb, *The Salmon Fisheries of the Pacific Coast* (Washington, D.C., 1911), Bureau of Fisheries Document No. 751; various issues of *Pacific Fisherman* and *Pacific Packers Report*.

Average and official prices paid gillnetters: Various issues of *Pacific Fisherman*; National Marine Fisheries Service (pers. comm.).

Consumer Price Index: U.S. Department of Labor, Bureau of Labor Statistics, *Handbook of Labor Statistics, 1972* (Washington, D.C., 1973), Bulletin No. 1790.

Index